THE TEENS ARE NOT ALRIGHT

ALSO BY CATHY VATTEROTT

Rethinking Grading: Meaningful Assessment for Standards-Based Learning

Rethinking Homework: Best Practices That Support Diverse Needs, 2nd Edition

THE TEENS ARE NOT ALRIGHT

School and Classroom Practices to Support Student Well-Being

Cathy Vatterott

Arlington, Virginia USA

2111 Wilson Boulevard, Suite 300 • Arlington, VA 22201 USA
Phone: 800-933-2723 or 703-578-9600
Website: www.ascd.org • Email: member@ascd.org
Author guidelines: www.ascd.org/write

Richard Culatta, *Chief Executive Officer;* Anthony Rebora, *Chief Content Officer;* Genny Ostertag, *Managing Director, Book Acquisitions & Editing;* Mary Beth Nielsen, *Director, Book Editing;* Miriam Calderone, *Editor;* Masie Chong, *Senior Graphic Designer;* Cynthia Stock, *Typesetter;* Kelly Marshall, *Production Manager;* Shajuan Martin, *E-Publishing Specialist*

Copyright © 2026 Cathy Vatterott. All rights reserved. It is illegal to reproduce copies of this work in print or electronic format (including reproductions displayed on a secure intranet or stored in a retrieval system or other electronic storage device from which copies can be made or displayed) without the prior written permission of the publisher. By purchasing only authorized electronic or print editions and not participating in or encouraging piracy of copyrighted materials, you support the rights of authors and publishers. Readers who wish to reproduce or republish excerpts of this work in print or electronic format may do so for a small fee by contacting the Copyright Clearance Center (CCC), 222 Rosewood Dr., Danvers, MA 01923, USA (phone: 978-750-8400; fax: 978-646-8600; web: www.copyright.com). To inquire about site licensing options or any other reuse, contact ASCD Permissions at www.ascd.org/permissions or permissions@ascd.org. For a list of vendors authorized to license ASCD ebooks to institutions, see www.ascd.org/epubs. Send translation inquiries to translations@ascd.org.

ASCD® is a registered trademark of Association for Supervision and Curriculum Development. All other trademarks contained in this book are the property of, and reserved by, their respective owners, and are used for editorial and informational purposes only. No such use should be construed to imply sponsorship or endorsement of the book by the respective owners.

All web links in this book are correct as of the publication date below but may have become inactive or otherwise modified since that time. If you notice a deactivated or changed link, please email books@ascd.org with the words "Link Update" in the subject line. In your message, please specify the web link, the book title, and the page number on which the link appears.

PAPERBACK ISBN: 978-1-4166-3408-9   ASCD product #126001   n12/25
PDF EBOOK ISBN: 978-1-4166-3409-6; see Books in Print for other formats.
Quantity discounts are available: email programteam@ascd.org or call 800-933-2723, ext. 5773, or 703-575-5773. For desk copies, go to www.ascd.org/deskcopy.

Library of Congress Cataloging-in-Publication Data is available for this title.
Library of Congress Control Number: 2025035393

---

35 34 33 32 31 30 29 28 27 26   1 2 3 4 5 6 7 8 9 10 11 12

For our teens:
May they experience joy
and calm, and may they have
the freedom to dream.

Preface ix
1. Cultural Influences on Teen Stress 1
2. The Stress of Adolescence 16
3. Why We Need a Paradigm Shift 30
4. The Less Stressful Classroom 45
5. Schoolwide Wellness Practices, Policies, and Programs 76
Afterword 107
Acknowledgments 109
References 111
Index 118
About the Author 123

Preface

I am not a mental health professional, yet I felt compelled to write this book about teen stress. I had a feeling in my gut that there had to be a better way forward for our students.

My concerns about teen stress began several years ago, while I was conducting professional development about effective homework practices. Most of the schools I worked with were in affluent communities, and I began hearing a worrisome message: Teachers were seeing a noticeable uptick in student stress (in both boys and girls) and perfectionism (especially among girls). Then I got the consulting job that set me on the course to write this book.

The school where I landed was the most exclusive independent high school I had ever worked with, serving very rich and very famous parents and their children. Several consultants had been brought in the day I was there, and the day ended with a student panel to talk about student stress. The students' voices cracked as they talked about being overscheduled, overloaded, sleep-deprived, and frantic. They said that they just wanted to make their parents proud. It broke my heart. What were we doing to these kids? Was school making their stress worse?

We know that stress is not just a problem for the children of the rich and famous. It's everywhere, and most educators have witnessed it firsthand. Child and adolescent mental health has been declared an urgent public health issue, and teen stress is a complex problem with many contributing cultural influences. To make matters worse, the physical, emotional, and social changes of adolescence coalesce with many of those cultural influences to exacerbate stress in teens. The practices in middle schools and high schools are often out of sync with the developmental needs of adolescents, thereby adding more strain to the already stressful time of adolescence.

As educators, we have tried our best to help. We have implemented numerous remedies, including social-emotional learning (SEL) to teach students vital life skills, and stress management approaches like mindfulness training and the use of therapy dogs. But we can't teach our way out of this crisis with the right SEL curriculum or solve the problem by treating the symptoms. We need to understand how school practices are contributing to the problem of teen stress—and then we need to make changes.

As an educator, you *can* have a significant impact on teen stress, and this book can help. I begin in Chapter 1 by outlining the mix of cultural factors that contribute to teen stress. In Chapter 2, I provide a crash course in adolescence to remind you of the significant life transition that it represents and the developmental needs that go with it. With that information in hand, we consider in Chapter 3 the shifts in practice that are needed to create a less stressful school, a less stressful classroom, and an environment that supports student well-being. In Chapter 4, we explore how schools can change students' day-to-day experience to meet their needs for autonomy and competence, both in and out of the classroom. Educators can allow students more input into school decisions that affect them, and we can free them to take charge of how they learn and how they show what they have learned. We can nurture their relationships with peers and teachers with intentional practices. Finally, Chapter 5 examines how to begin the process of developing a comprehensive mental health support system.

Throughout the book, I feature quotes and examples from educators, parents, and students I have worked with or interviewed to further illuminate my findings and my thoughts.

With the help of this book, you can begin to make changes that will support your adolescent students' well-being and reduce their stress.

Cultural Influences on Teen Stress

In 2021, the teen mental health crisis got real. After years of cover stories and increasingly troubling statistics, the trauma of a global pandemic elevated the situation to the forefront of America's attention. Once the COVID-19 pandemic had escalated a long-smoldering problem into a four-alarm fire, the depth and severity of teen distress could no longer be ignored.

Within a three-month period, four well-respected medical organizations sounded the alarm. In October 2021, the American Academy of Pediatrics, the American Academy of Child and Adolescent Psychiatry, and the Children's Hospital Association issued a joint declaration of a national emergency in child and adolescent mental health (American Academy of Pediatrics, 2021). And in December 2021, the U.S. Surgeon General issued an advisory titled *Protecting Youth Mental Health* calling attention to "an urgent public health issue" (p. 5) and offering extensive recommendations for young people, families, educators, and members of the medical and mental health communities.

Since 2021, the epidemic of youth mental health disorders has continued. It is a problem that predates the pandemic and has been steadily worsening for years. In fact, youth mental health has been declining continuously since the 1950s (Twenge et al., 2010), but the statistics in the last two decades have been particularly troublesome:

- Between 2008 and 2017, major depression for youth ages 12 to 17 increased by 52 percent (from 8.7 percent to 13.2 percent), and it rose by 63 percent (from 8.1 percent to 13.2 percent) in young adults ages 18 to 25 (Twenge et al., 2019).
- From 2009 to 2019, one in three high school students and one in two female students reported persistent feelings of sadness or hopelessness, an overall increase of 40 percent from 2009 (Centers for Disease Control and Prevention [CDC], 2019).
- Between 2011 and 2015, youth psychiatric visits to emergency departments for depression, anxiety, and behavioral challenges increased by 28 percent (U.S. Surgeon General, 2021).
- From 2010 to 2020, emergency room visits for 10–14-year-olds for nonfatal self-harm increased by 48 percent for boys and 188 percent for girls (Haidt, 2024).
- Suicide rates for 10–14-year-olds have increased since 2010. In 2022, suicide was the second leading cause of death for 10–14-year-olds, and the third leading cause of death for individuals between the ages of 15 and 24 (National Institute of Mental Health, 2022).
- Children from affluent families have consistently been shown to have the highest rates of depression and anxiety disorders of any group of children in the United States (Abeles, 2015; Fullan, 2021; Levine, 2006).

Although it is possible that increased awareness and diagnoses of mental health problems have led to a corresponding increase in reports, experts suspect that statistics are underreported, since many adolescents and their families do not seek help. Any way you look at them, these statistics are troubling. What could be driving this rise in teen mental health problems?

Plenty of pundits and members of the general public would like to point to a single cause (say, smartphones), which would lead to a straightforward solution. But that would be an oversimplification and wishful thinking. As in the parable of the blind men and the elephant, in which each man feels a different part of the animal and comes away with a completely different understanding of what is in front of him, it's easy to fixate on one part of something and think you see the whole picture. Adolescent mental health is a complex problem, and there are no simple solutions to complex problems.

In reality, the current mental health crisis in teens stems from the interplay of cultural changes that have occurred in the United States during the last two to four decades. Rather than there being one primary culprit, the growing consensus among mental health experts is that a number of social and cultural forces have converged to produce the harmful milieu in which teen stress grows, including media overload, smartphones and social media, parenting trends, the wealth gap and achievement culture, and the college admissions industry. All of these contribute to the complex issue of child and adolescent mental health. It's not *one* thing, it's *everything*.

The World Teens Live in: Media Overload

The world teens live in is stress-inducing for three reasons: the events and problems of the world, the reporting of the events and problems of the world, and the instant access to information that the internet allows. The current generation of teens has never known a world without terrorism, school shootings, smartphones, or the 24-hour news cycle. Whether they're discrete disasters happening throughout the world or chronic global problems such as intolerance, violence, war, poverty, and the climate crisis, all these weigh heavy on a young person's mind. But the way the events and problems of the world are reported makes them even worse. CNN debuted as the first 24-hour all-news channel in 1980, followed by CNBC in 1989 and MSNBC and Fox in 1996, all providing live coverage of events and breaking news. The 24-hour news cycle is stress-inducing in itself, as media outlets have the time and opportunity to expand their coverage of stories to feature every possible angle and every eyewitness, and to loop those stories over and over to fill those 24 hours. It has become relatively simple to conduct in-depth, unrelenting coverage of outlier stories of tragic accidents, natural disasters, gruesome murders, and horrific wars around the world. As the saying in news goes, "If it bleeds, it leads."

Both the selection of outlier stories and the grim narratives that come with them reveal a "bad news bias" (Thompson, 2022). The looping of stories of calamitous or aberrant events makes those events seem more prevalent than they really are, leading anxious teens to feel as though there is always something to worry about. Even if an event occurs thousands of miles away, the immediate notification leads teens to feel like it's right in their own backyard. To make matters worse, every story comes with video, connecting much more viscerally than words alone and easily shared on social media, often with disturbing images that stick in one's mind.

The hyperconnectedness of social media not only leaves teens overexposed to all sorts of national and world events but also makes it hard to escape the news. Their online world and the real world blur together as one. As one researcher described it, "they're in a cauldron of stimulus that they can't get away from, or don't want to get away from, or don't know how to get away from" (Schrobsdorff, 2016, p. 47.)

Smartphones and Social Media

For teens, their phone is a big part of their world. It's their portal to their social life, connecting them with their friends and online communities of like-minded peers. It plays their music, affirms their identity, and is an instant boredom buster. But it can be an all-consuming part of their life as well. The average teen gets 237 notifications daily and spends nearly *five hours a day* on social media platforms like YouTube, TikTok, Instagram, and Snapchat (DeAngelis, 2024; Faverio & Sidoti, 2024; Langreo & Prothero, 2025).

Of all the possible contributors to the teen mental health crisis, none has garnered more public attention than phones, with many people believing the smartphone is *the* culprit. That belief has been reinforced by Jonathan Haidt's (2024) bestselling book *The Anxious Generation: How the Great Rewiring of Childhood Is Causing an Epidemic of Mental Illness* (2024). Haidt takes a deep dive into the evolution of smartphone technology and paints an ominous, sometimes overly dramatic picture of the effects smartphones have on our children's mental health. Although smartphones are not the boogeyman, Haidt does offer well-researched and compelling correlations—things that make you go "hmm." Here are a few of his findings:

- Citing Twenge (2018), Haidt notes that teen anxiety and depression began to rise after 2012, when the majority of Americans owned a smartphone.
- The oldest members of Generation Z began puberty around 2009—the same year Facebook introduced the "like" button and Twitter introduced the "retweet" button. These pivotal changes made it easy to judge and be judged.
- In 2010, the first phones with front-facing cameras arrived, making it easier to take photos and videos of oneself. Instagram, which also launched in 2010, made it easy to post carefully curated photos and videos.
- The more enamored teens became with social media, the more time-consuming it became for them to orchestrate their online images. The more popular social media became, the more essential it became for teens' social survival.

These conclusions about the cultural impact of smartphones and social media seem reasonable. Two other claims by Haidt (2024) seem a bit over the top:

- Smartphones have been made so appealing to children and adolescents that they reduce interest in all non-screen-based experiences.
- Smartphones can cause social deprivation, sleep deprivation, attention fragmentation, and addiction.

Although any of these statements may be true for *some* teens in extreme cases, it is questionable whether they are true for *all* teens. Thompson (2022) offers a more nuanced view:

> Social media isn't like rat poison, which is toxic to almost everyone. It's more like alcohol: a mildly addictive substance that can enhance social situations but can also lead to dependency and depression among a minority of users.

The two most pervasive problems of social media for teens come down to their developing identity and self-esteem. First, adolescent identity is still a work in progress and is easily influenced. Social media and popular culture bombard teens with airbrushed images of perfection and messages that erode their sense of self-worth, telling them they are not good-looking enough, popular enough, smart enough, or rich enough (U.S. Surgeon General, 2021).

The second hazard is that while teens have always stumbled socially on occasion, nowadays any social misstep can be immediately documented (everyone has a camera) and broadcast to a large community (often anonymously). No wonder teens are anxious. The interplay between the technology and the emotional and social needs of teens comes at a time when kids' self-esteem is fragile and they are most vulnerable to peer approval. Perhaps teens' unique vulnerability is why schools that have gone phone-free have seen engagement in the classroom improve and discipline problems such as fights, bullying, and drug-related offenses decrease (Banerji, 2025).

Parenting Trends

If we were to take our cues from a certain school of experts, we would think that bad parenting was the primary cause of "what's the matter with kids today." Derisively referred to as "helicopter parenting" (as in hovering) or "bulldozer parenting" (as in clearing the path of all obstacles), modern parenting practices are often blamed for the epidemic of stressed-out children. Research hardly bears out how common overparenting is, but researchers have found that overcontrolling parenting can negatively affect children and adolescents' well-being (American Psychological Association [APA], 2018).

Psychologists and family therapists believe that parental trends of overprotecting or overdirecting are actually fear based—and, in defense of parents, much of that fear is media driven. The rise of fear-based parenting began in the early 1980s, around the same time CNN debuted. Fed by the bad news bias, repetitive looping of outlier stories about harm to children (such as child abductions and freak accidents) stoked fear in parents about their children's safety (Lythcott-Haims, 2015). Lahey (2015) observes,

> [I]f we are to believe the fear-mongering mass media, that harm is all around us. Baby snatchers disguised as maternity nurses, antibiotic-resistant germs, toxic chemicals, disease-carrying ticks, bullying kids, unfair teachers, murderous school shooters... no wonder we've gone nuts where our children are concerned. (p. xiv)

All parents instinctively protect their children from harm, but when that harm has been exaggerated, the parental response can be out of proportion to the true threat. Parenting from fear, even with the best intentions, can morph from protecting a child from physical danger to shielding them from failure, frustration, embarrassment, or feelings of discomfort or disappointment. This overprotection shows up at school when a parent delivers a forgotten homework assignment or calls the teacher to ask why the grade hasn't been posted yet for the test the student just completed.

In addition to fear-based overprotection, parents' reactions to events can either precipitate anxiety in their children or ease it. Children of all ages take their emotional cues from parents. If a child's mother is deathly afraid of dogs, the child trusts that their mother is right—there must be a reason to fear dogs. If an anxious parent reacts with alarm to a failed exam, it's easy for a teenager to adopt that same sense of alarm ("Yikes, this must be a really big deal!"). Parental anxiety is contagious, and so is calm.

Psychologists now believe that overprotecting children hampers the natural course of their development of independence and resilience (APA, 2018). Would a child ever learn to ride a bike if they were never allowed to fall? When overprotected children reach adolescence, they often have trouble coping with failure, because they haven't had any practice (Lahey, 2015). The more children have been protected and rescued, the fewer strategies they develop to solve their own problems, self-soothe, cope with uncomfortable feelings, or manage negative emotions.

When all barriers have been removed for them, children lack experience in working through obstacles, leading them to feel less competent to solve problems and have less confidence in themselves. All this leads to a vicious circle: Children don't trust their own decisions, which can make them anxious, which then makes it easy for a parent to rescue them from that uncomfortable feeling, thus reinforcing the child's feeling of incompetence. As parents, the less we trust our children to make decisions and possibly fail, the less they trust themselves (Lahey, 2015).

The Decline of Independent Play

Many parents today believe their job is to engage their child in as many structured activities as possible, from as early an age as possible, to build aptitudes and skills. Those structured activities can lead to an overscheduled child and may crowd out another important activity for well-being: play.

Leading play researchers point to a significant decline in free play as an overlooked factor in children's declining mental health (Gray et al., 2023). They speculate that independent, in-person play has been diminished by an increase in structured enrichment activities, homework load, and phone-based interactions.

What counts as play? Researchers define play as self-directed, freely chosen activities away from adult oversight and intervention, that participants engage in because they want to—not to achieve some end. For adolescents, play is the difference between a jam session and a music performance, or a game of pick-up basketball and a competition against another team.

Why is play important to well-being? Play is nature's way of developing social skills like negotiation, conflict resolution, emotional regulation, and empathy. Play helps children develop resilience and confidence, leading to a decrease in anxiety (Haidt, 2024). Play, in other words, is a natural, organic approach to social-emotional learning.

The Wealth Gap and Achievement Culture

The widening of the wealth gap is another societal shift that has exacerbated teen stress. During the last 50 years, the share of the United States' aggregate income going to the top 1 percent has more than doubled, while the share going to middle- and lower-income households has fallen

(Horowitz et al., 2020; Vatterott, 2018). The middle class has shrunk, as the rich have gotten richer and the poor have gotten poorer. The wealth gap creates two different scenarios within families, leading to two different kinds of stress for teens.

Teens Living in Poverty

The stresses of living in or near poverty have been well documented: Food insecurity, housing insecurity, unstable employment, and financial concerns loom large. Teens living in poverty often have to balance school and homework with family responsibilities like cooking or caring for younger siblings, in addition to taking on part-time or even full-time work to make ends meet. Adolescents living in poverty may be juggling school responsibilities with those of being responsible wage earners, adding more stress to their lives (Hall, 2019).

Urban and rural adolescents living in poverty share similar burdens. Both are more likely to experience poor mental health owing to past adverse childhood experiences (Crouch et al., 2020; Melito-Connors, 2024). Both urban and rural adolescents may have limited access to quality health care, with mental health care often even less accessible. Although urban teens living in poverty are more likely to have lost a friend or family member to crime or gun violence, rural teens living in poverty see more deaths by drug overdose and are at a greater risk for suicide than their urban counterparts (Hall, 2019; National Institutes of Health, 2020).

Growing up in poverty also weighs heavily on a teen's decisions about their future, with responsibility to their family adding additional stress. Teens may be forced to put their own plans on hold to help provide for their family, or they may feel an obligation to succeed in college or a career as a way to lift their family out of poverty. So whether adolescents are living in rural or urban areas, they come to school with a second "invisible backpack" of stress (Melito-Connors, 2024).

Teens in Affluent Families and the Achievement Culture

For affluent families, the shrinking of the middle class has made it seem as though there are only two destinations in life for their children—wealth or poverty. This apparent dichotomy has led to a fear among many affluent parents that their children will end up on the wrong side of that divide (Miller, 2018). The increasing income gap has led to *status insecurity,* or a fear of not maintaining one's advantaged position in society. A fierce survivalist mindset, however irrational, has emerged among some families to protect the privilege they are fortunate enough to have. As this mindset became more widespread, what is now known as the *achievement culture* or *academic obsession* (Fullan, 2021) was born.

Those with the achievement culture mindset hold the singular belief that the Ivy League is *the* ticket to success, the only way to secure a child's future. This binary mindset has been labeled by some sardonically as "Harvard or homeless," or "Yale or jail" (Bruni, 2016). As one psychologist put it, "Parents are worried that if their children don't get into Harvard, they're going to be standing with a tin cup on the corner somewhere" (Novotney, 2009, p. 2). For adolescents, often naïve about how the world works, it's easy to believe their parents must be right—that the path to a successful life is narrow and that the right path can remove all uncertainty about their future.

The achievement culture is a behemoth that permeates families and communities and creates stress in teens by defining future success very narrowly. With the help of social media, communities increasingly segregated by income, and success stories of young people with Ivy credentials landing prestigious jobs, the narrative of the achievement culture has developed: Attending an elite college = wealth and power = success = happiness in life. That groupthink often gets reinforced by the life experience of parents who attended an elite college, have garnered wealth and power, and are seemingly successful and happy. This belief system is often reinforced by community values and a form of collective anxiety ("Your son hasn't applied to colleges yet?!" "Where is your daughter going?"). Add to this mixture the ubiquitous bragging by parents whose children were accepted by Ivy League schools, and it becomes like a social contagion.

Teens are equally influenced by their peers and social media, buying into some common narratives: If you are smart, you belong at an Ivy school, and "if you don't get in, you're a loser with no future," as a college counselor told me one teen put it. Teens also often make the faulty assumption that a low acceptance rate correlates with a superior education. This black-and-white thinking is characteristic of adolescent thought processes in general. Add to this mindset the obligation teens feel to their parents—"I just want to make my parents proud"—and the fear of being a disappointment piles on more stress.

The College Admissions Industry: A Willing Accomplice

The growth of the achievement culture has had help. The college admissions industry willingly keeps alive the dream that admission to an elite college is the ticket to lifelong success and security. It has exploited and profited from families' fear of losing their social position and has helped disseminate the myth that an Ivy League education is the path to financial privilege. After all, what would you do (or pay) to assure your child's financial security in the future? This myth has been perpetuated by college admissions industry processes, which encourage students to apply to numerous schools, leading to a deluge of applications for each school. This practice creates an artificial scarcity of slots that allows schools to tout the small percentage of actual acceptances, creating the illusion of exclusivity (Bruni, 2016). As Brooks (2024) points out,

> Universities came to realize that the more people they reject, the more their cachet soars. Some of these rejection academies run marketing campaigns to lure more and more applicants—and then brag about turning away 96 percent of them. (p. 28)

This artificial scarcity has been further incentivized by the annual Best Colleges ratings of *U.S. News & World Report*. A lower acceptance rate earns a college a higher rating. This creates a perverse incentive for colleges to develop intensive marketing processes, because more applications lead to more rejections, which lead to higher ratings (Brooks, 2024; Bruni, 2016). The illusion of exclusivity feeds students' insecurity and belief that they must submit multiple applications to improve the odds—a sort of lottery mentality—and the cycle continues.

For many students, the solution is to orchestrate their four-year high school course schedule and extracurriculars strictly for the purpose of college admission, which is antithetical to what adolescents need to develop their identity. What happened to teens' freedom to explore their interests or find their passion through electives and extracurricular activities?

The competitiveness of college admissions leads many to the conclusion that the more students can do, the better—more activities, more advanced placement (AP) classes, more test prep, more attempts at the SAT. In many high-achieving schools, there is almost a superstition among parents, students, and teachers that straying from the de facto formula of multiple AP classes and activities and intensive SAT prep and multiple retakes will lead to catastrophic results (Vatterott, 2019). Teachers and administrators see a common pattern among anxious students:

> They *want* to be in all these activities and take all these AP classes, and then they get stressed out because they are overscheduled. They act like they've got it all together, then the smallest thing has them in tears or leads to a meltdown. . . . There's this hypercompetitiveness, that if you're not *the best,* you're nothing. . . . And heaven forbid they get a *B* on something. To them, it may as well be an *F.* (Vatterott, 2019, p. 14)

The achievement culture has spawned a multi-billion-dollar industry of college consultants. There are currently about 10,000 of them in the United States, up from fewer than 100 in 1990 (Goldstein & Healy, 2019). College consultants offer guidance on selecting high school courses and extracurriculars, SAT and ACT test prep, writing college application essays, and perfecting the college application. Some students and parents have so fully bought into the achievement culture that they come to the college consultant confident the student will be admitted into an Ivy League school. After all, they have followed the formula—they have done everything right in their little pond. It can be a rude awakening to discover that, after all that work, there are no promises.

If students and parents are lucky, they have an ethical college consultant who is honest from the beginning about the odds of college admissions and who does their best to match the student with the best-fitting college. Unfortunately, the industry is not regulated, leaving some consultants to ignore optional ethical guidelines established by national professional associations such as those from the National Association for College Admission Counseling (2024).

For parents of considerable wealth, the sky is the limit. The hottest guru in college consulting, Jamie Beaton, says he has cracked the code to getting students into one of a handful of elite colleges. For $200,000, he offers a four- to six-year program, starting as early as middle school. His secret is to "optimize childhood by starting to build skills and interests in the years before high school" (Belkin, 2024). His program includes tutoring as well as advice on how to secure teacher recommendations and build up extracurriculars, including publishing research papers, writing a book, or starting a podcast.

"Optimizing childhood" is one approach. Then there is a different kind of college consultant. Jaime Caryl-Klika is an independent educational consultant with more than 25 years of experience in both college counseling and college admissions. She is a professional member of the Independent Educational Consultants Association, considered the gold standard in the profession. She is also a certified educational planner, the highest credential in the profession and one held by fewer than 300 educational consultants worldwide. Her mission is to help students and parents find the college that is the best fit for them, and to make the process exciting rather than stressful. Much of her job is managing expectations. She strongly suggests that all her clients read Frank Bruni's *Where You Go Is Not Who You'll Be: An Antidote to the College Admissions Mania* (2016). She works with students to balance their lists of schools in terms of selectivity and encourages them to look beyond schools that reject more than 90 percent of applicants to schools that offer the same opportunities yet are much more accessible in terms of admissions. When asked, "What are some of the more stressful aspects of the college application process for students?" Caryl-Klika replied:

> Sometimes the parent-child relationship can be consumed by the college application process and students often feel as though it's all parents talk and care about. I encourage families to compartmentalize the conversation and reserve one day per week to talk about all things college. . . . The most stressful part of parental involvement comes when the student has worked hard on their college essay, the parents read it, and then say it's not good enough or edit it with a very heavy hand. (personal communication, March 14, 2025)

The achievement culture is pervasive in middle-income families as well as affluent ones. Pity the family of lesser means who can't afford the college consultant and must rely on the overworked school counselors for guidance. If the family can afford college at all, the cost is often steep—so the answer becomes, beef up the high school résumé, take the AP classes, get the grades to get the scholarship to get into college, and hope for additional financial aid. No matter which economic class a family belongs to, they have that nagging feeling that they can never do enough to increase the odds of admission to the right school (Bruni, 2016).

"It's a game," one parent told me, but they feel powerless to control it or are afraid to do anything less. This game is damaging to teens. As Flanagan (2021) puts it, "This is a system that screws the poor, hollows out the middle class, and turns rich kids into exhausted, anxious, and maximally stressed-out adolescents who believe their future depends on getting into one of a very small group of colleges that routinely reject upwards of 90 percent of their applicants" (p. 54).

But parents and students can opt out of this game, if only they have the courage to go against the prevailing norms in their community. Then the process can be a joyful and meaningful journey. There are thousands of colleges and universities that may prove a perfect fit for many students, and there are also numerous paths to becoming a successful, well-adjusted, and happy adult. A recent survey (American Student Assistance, 2025) shows that teen interest is growing in alternative paths to college, such as trade or technical schools and apprenticeships.

Schools Caught in the Middle

In some affluent communities, the ultimate academic obsession begins early as parents vie for coveted spots in exclusive preschools, a process dubbed the "rug rat race" by one pair of researchers (Ramey & Ramey, 2009). Again, parents feel they can never do enough to improve the odds. The rug rat race often leads families of means to pay extravagant tuition for exclusive private schools based on the percentage of alumni who eventually go on to attend elite colleges.

Both public and private high schools have become unwitting and often unwilling accomplices to the achievement culture, judged by the extent of their college prep curricula and their Ivy League acceptance rates. In most school districts, the residents of the community elect the members of the school board, which is expected to reflect the values of the community. High school administrators may then be pressured by board members or other influential community members to accommodate the wishes of parents ("Yes, your daughter can take five AP classes this year"), creating tension between what is best for students and what the community demands. It's a delicate balancing act between satisfying parents and safeguarding the well-being of students.

Schools do have ways to opt out of certain aspects of the achievement culture. Some schools limit AP courses during the junior year or permit students to take no more than three AP courses each year. The high school profile that goes forward with the student transcript informs admissions officers of these policies, and colleges cannot penalize students for them.

Of all the cultural forces discussed in this chapter, academic obsession is the most damaging to teens. It changes who they are, kills joy, and robs them of what should be a carefree adolescence. It turns teens into rudderless box checkers: four AP classes, check; debate team, check; two sports, check; honor roll, check. This relentless focus on achievement crowds out the important psychological needs of teens (Vatterott, 2019).

Conclusion

To combat all the social and cultural forces that contribute to teen stress, we must first understand and respect the developmental needs of adolescents. All these stressors are occurring while teens are experiencing the unique physical and emotional changes of adolescence. Under these conditions, handling stress is especially difficult—more challenging than it is for adults. Chapter 2 explores these changes and their ramifications.

2

The Stress of Adolescence

As if the world wasn't stressful enough, adolescents are also in the middle of a significant life transition. Middle and high school students are experiencing profound physical, cognitive, and emotional shifts, matched only by the developmental changes that happen from birth to age 3. These changes are stressors by themselves and complicate teens' ability to manage additional stress. Adolescents also have strong developmental needs for establishing their identity and competence, and resolving those needs is the essential job of adolescence. Unfortunately, this process takes place within a highly sensitive body and a maturing brain under construction. These confines of biology make everything harder.

Body Biology During Adolescence

Biology may not be destiny, but it sure can complicate a teen's life. The physical changes of puberty and fluctuating hormones cause adolescent bodies and brains to be more sensitive to the physical influences of nutrition, sleep, and exercise, all of which affect mood and the ability to tolerate stress. At a time when parents appropriately give teens the freedom to manage their own diet and sleep habits, teens often choose to push the boundaries of both. It's easy to turn to stimulants such as energy drinks, sugar, and junk food to alter their energy level or mood. The power of healthy habits to mitigate stress during adolescence cannot be overstated.

The Biology of Sleep

The adolescent brain and body are going through extensive changes, and many of these changes are happening during sleep (Suni, 2023). The CDC (2024) and the National Sleep Foundation (2024) recommend 8–10 hours of sleep a night for teens ages 13–18, yet most of them clock in well below that. About 60 percent of middle schoolers and about 70 percent of high schoolers get an inadequate amount of sleep on school nights (CDC, 2024). One contributing factor is the blue light from smartphones, tablets, and computers. Exposure to this light even two hours before bedtime slows the body's release of the hormone melatonin, making it harder to fall asleep (National Sleep Foundation, 2022). And let's not forget the caffeine teens consume during the day to keep them awake because they didn't get enough sleep the night before, which then keeps them up the next night, and so on.

Some powerful research (Samuels, 2020) has recently emerged about the relationship between sleep and teens' ability to cope with stress. There is a vicious circle of sleep deprivation and mood disorders: Lack of sleep exacerbates anxiety and depression, and anxiety and depression interfere with sleep. As if that weren't enough, sleep deprivation affects executive functioning, problem solving, and decision making. The same study found that teens who got longer and higher-quality sleep ruminated less, had better active coping skills, and showed better academic performance.

Biology is one culprit here: During puberty, changes occur in the circadian rhythms that biologically program teens to stay awake later (National Research Council et al., 2000). When those sleep patterns are out of sync with school start times, teens end up more sleep deprived, feeding the vicious circle of anxiety and depression. An increasing number of secondary schools are starting school later in an effort to address this problem.

Brain Biology During Adolescence

Brain research further informs us about what's going on physiologically in the teen brain. A look at recent findings about adolescent brain development reveals the role of the developing brain in teen anxiety.

The Brain Under Construction

As the brain matures during adolescence, it undergoes *pruning,* a process that eliminates unused synapses to make the brain more efficient. But the timing of that pruning differs broadly by brain region. The limbic system, also known as the "emotional brain," finishes developing around puberty. The last part of the brain to be pruned is in the prefrontal cortex—the area of the brain responsible for the executive functions of planning, making decisions, setting priorities, forming strategies, and inhibiting impulses and inappropriate behavior. Unfortunately, this part of the brain is "under construction" in late adolescence and even into the 20s (Stixrud & Johnson, 2018).

So, although teens are mentally capable of thinking rationally in the absence of emotion or social pressure, the prefrontal cortex can easily be hijacked by the emotional brain. This makes it easy for teens to be impulsive and make unwise decisions:

> It might be helpful to think of the limbic system as an accelerator propelling a car along the highway, and the prefrontal cortex as the car's steering wheel and brakes. Because of the gap in the timing of the development of these two systems, adolescence is a time when the accelerator is being pushed down to the floor while the brakes have yet to be fully installed. (Armstrong, 2016, p. 10)

Teens are also biochemically more sensitive to stress because of fluctuations of neurotransmitters such as dopamine and serotonin (sometimes known as "feel-good chemicals" because they play an important role in mood regulation) and higher levels of the stress hormone cortisol (Armstrong, 2016).

Something else happens cognitively to adolescents: As part of their intellectual development, they are transitioning from being concrete thinkers to abstract thinkers. Concrete thinking—believing that everything is black or white, good or bad—gives way to more nuanced thinking (Vatterott, 2007). As teens gain the capacity for abstract thought, they can consider multiple possibilities leading to an infinite number of "what ifs." Unfortunately, the natural result of this new ability is the potential to ruminate over the serious and the mundane alike (Steinberg, 2017). Add this to the tendency of the emotional brain to take over in times of stress, and it is easy for teens to catastrophize events.

All these physical, cognitive, and neurological changes occur in concert, interact with one another, and make anxiety an easy emotion to access. And teens have a lot to be anxious about as they struggle to meet the unique developmental needs of adolescence—often with little downtime to do so.

The Importance of Developmental Needs

Developmentally, there are tasks all children need to accomplish at particular stages in their lives. Just as toddlers need to master walking and feeding themselves, adolescents need to accomplish several tasks in their transition to adulthood. Developmental tasks of adolescents include finding their unique identity and competencies, determining their moral values and belief systems, developing stable and productive peer relationships, and gaining independence from their parents. As adolescents are driven to resolve these developmental needs, they also have basic *human* needs for autonomy, power and freedom, love and belonging, and a sense of connectedness to others (Glasser, 1992; Steinberg, 2017).

The confluence of these needs and the compulsion to resolve them led developmental psychologist Erik Erikson to recommend a *psychosocial moratorium* for adolescents—a timeout from excessive responsibilities to allow them the freedom to reflect (Steinberg, 2017). For younger children, many parents and teachers say, "Let kids be kids," and they prioritize play. Teens, too, need unstructured time to just be teens, to form their identities, values, and views of the world.

Identity: The Central Theme of Adolescence

The most prominent of all the developmental needs of adolescence is the search for identity. Adolescents are beginning the lifelong process of figuring out who they are, what they believe, what their values and passions are, and what they want out of life (Klein, 2021). This is the time to embrace dreams and ambitions and to reflect on the infinite number of paths one's life could take. The search for identity is a deeply personal internal process, so it is natural for teens to be self-absorbed and somewhat egocentric. The question "Who am I?" demands time and space for reflection and gets especially complicated for teens who are grappling with gender identity, sexual orientation, or racial, ethnic, cultural, or religious identity.

Coming to terms with one's racial or ethnic identity can bring up a number of conflicts for teens. Do they embrace their racial identity or run away from it? How do they respond to stereotyping of their race or ethnicity (such as people assuming Asian students are good at math)? Multiracial identity can present its own unique challenges. Teens who are adopted may have little information about their racial or ethnic heritage, or they may have parents whose heritage differs from theirs, further complicating their search for identity. For teens who are questioning their gender identity, their dilemma becomes, "Who do I say I am when I'm still figuring it out myself? Do I fit into any category at all?" For teens who know they are gay, lesbian, or bisexual, other decisions need to be made—whether to hide or reveal their identity, whom it is safe to come out to, and how and when to do so. The most compelling problem for these teens is how to feel good about themselves when so many people are telling them it is wrong to be who they are.

Finding Their Islands of Competence

Part of teens' search for identity is finding what psychologists call their *islands of competence* (Brooks & Goldstein, 2001). Adolescents need to discover what they are good at by exploring and experimenting with a variety of activities. School is the most logical place to experience competence—to be a good student, a good athlete, or at least good at a particular subject. But if a teen is not a strong student and not good at sports, they need other opportunities for competence. It is important that teens achieve competence at *something*, whether it be academics, athletics, music, art, extracurricular activities, hobbies, or work.

Searching for one's identity, sense of competence, and social position often leads to fragile self-esteem, especially in girls (Steinberg, 2017). Struggling to make sense of it all makes for a very busy teen brain. There is a lot to figure out, all while the brain is under construction and highly reactive, making this search an intellectually and emotionally taxing job.

To complicate a teen's life even further, these developmental challenges do not take place in a vacuum. Developing identity and discovering competence are social as well as mental processes. Teens attempt to meet these and other developmental needs through their experiences with others as they navigate the four worlds they live in:

- The world of parental expectations and values
- The world of peers
- The virtual world
- The world of school

Each of the worlds teens live in presents different avenues through which teens understand themselves, and each is integrally linked to the others. A teen's identity as a student is related to their identity as a peer, as a friend, as a family member, and as a member of the community (Klein, 2021). The messages of each world intersect and influence one another, getting jumbled up in a teen's head as they try to make sense of the larger outside world and their place in it. Each world has the potential to make adolescence more or less stressful, to add to stresses from the other worlds or to help moderate them. In every world, teens are bombarded with messages: People tell them who they are, who they should be, how to feel, and what to think. As they struggle to figure out who they are and what they are good at, teens get many conflicting messages about who they are *supposed* to be and what it's *important* to be good at, based on what others value and reward. Those messages may or may not be in sync with what they believe about themselves, further complicating their ability to define themselves. With all this inflow, teens often can't hear themselves think. When it comes to figuring out who they are, the inside of a teen's head can get noisy and confusing (see Figure 2.1).

Figure 2.1
The World Inside a Teen's Head

As teens reflect on their competencies, they look to the messages from each world to tell them what they are good at, which brings more questions. Who decides what success or failure is? Are all competencies equally valued by others? In a highly competitive community, does it matter if you are *good* at something or only if you are the *best*? A teen may be good at helping people, be a great chess player, or have a green thumb, but they may not perceive it as "something I am good at" if it is not validated by others. The experiences teens have in these worlds change them as they form their identities and clarify their values. They make decisions about who they are, what's right and wrong, and whether they should trust others' perceptions. As teens interact with the four worlds, they interpret, internalize, and integrate messages about who they should be into their formative identity.

The World of Parental Expectations and Values

As part of their transition to adulthood, adolescents need to detach from their parents and learn to function independently. Gaining independence is an important developmental task in forming their unique identity. To accomplish this, adolescents must renegotiate relationships with their parents or other adults serving in a parental role.

The parent-child relationship is complex. As anyone who has raised (or been) a teenager knows, there are internal tensions between adolescent developmental needs and the parent-child relationship. Although adolescents are striving to gain independence from their parents, they still need them for emotional and financial support. As teens attempt to become their own person, they still need the unconditional love, acceptance, and approval of their parents, and most feel an obligation to please their parents. This is where parenting an adolescent gets especially complicated.

Teens are rarely in the dark about what their parents value, whether it is achievement, competition, money, family, faith, service to the community, altruism, or intellectual curiosity. The conflict for teens arises as they reflect on these questions: "Do I have to be who my parents want me to be? Do I have to follow the path they define for me, or do I get to have my own dream?" Most parents want their child to chart their own course in life (eventually), but they may not be clearly communicating that sentiment. Parents' messages can easily be misperceived by the adolescent brain, which is still transitioning from concrete to abstract thinking and may interpret things as black and white, right or wrong, success or failure.

Even when they have the best intentions, parents may not always realize the message they convey or the anxiety they reveal about their child's future. What parents mean to say and what teens hear are often two very different things. For instance, parents rightfully want their children to work hard and do their best in school. But when parents ask, "How did you end up with a *B* in that class?" their teen may hear, "An *A* is the only acceptable grade; a *B* may as well be an *F*." If parents exclaim, "I can't believe you're not the starting quarterback!" their teen may hear, "If you're not the best, you're a failure" (Pope, 2016). Because perception is reality to adolescents, the message and the way it's perceived is crucial.

The phenomenon of the achievement culture discussed in Chapter 1 can add another layer of stress for both parents and teens. Not surprisingly, teens today report that they are under more pressure from parents than in the past (Challenge Success & NBC News, 2021). Parents who are nervous about their child's future often reflexively focus on grades, athletics, or feeding the college résumé as a remedy for their own anxiety. The danger in this focus is how often it is misperceived by teens.

Parents' overemphasis on achievement can interfere with their children's development of identity, leading teens to falsely believe, "Oh, that's who I am" and "I am nothing without my achievements." These beliefs can lead to the misperception of parental love as *conditional love* (Levine, 2006). When teens are in this labyrinth of misperceptions, they may feel as though "they only love me *if* ___." So they tell themselves the story that "my parents will only love me if I have a perfect GPA/I'm the star of the team/I get the scholarship." Because they still need the approval and love of their parents, they may put excessive pressure on themselves. In the words of one teen from a student panel on stress, "I just want to make them proud." As Levine (2006) observes, "When parents place an excessively high value on outstanding performance, children come to see anything less than perfection as failure" (p. 29).

Unfortunately, placing one's entire identity and self-esteem in one basket can lead to *maladaptive perfectionism*—perfectionism that impairs functioning. Teens who already lean toward perfectionism may see achievements as their only path to competence and often tell themselves that they must be good at everything or else be a failure. Girls seem especially susceptible to the feeling that they must do it all, excelling at "both traditional 'male' standards (achievement, accomplishments, good grades, and high powered careers) as well as traditional 'female' standards (being thin, pretty, and wearing nice clothes)" (Levine, 2006, p. 178). Holding oneself to such unrealistic standards is exhausting and stress-inducing.

If the achievement culture is pervasive in a student's community, this stress is compounded by other adults. One superintendent in an affluent community told me wryly, "There are three career paths for our students—doctor, lawyer, and unsuccessful." Parents' friends, teachers, coaches, and relatives are all poised to offer well-meaning advice about college, careers, and which life path is the best. The persistent questions "What are your plans? Where have you applied to?" precipitate an air of collective anxiety. If this is all adolescents hear from adults, the voices in their head are loud and the pressure they put on themselves is palpable.

Teens often hear that grades, test scores, and college admissions are high-stakes decisions (*don't screw this up!*). Based on what metric? That admission to the elite college = success = happiness? There is a sense that students' future success or failure hangs in the balance with each exam, each grade, each college application. Being told that college admission is the most important decision in their life and that they must make it at the age of 15 is harrowing, to say the least. As if that narrative weren't stressful enough, it comes at a time when, due to their ongoing cognitive transition to abstract thinking, teens are often ill equipped to make decisions about such long-range plans.

The World of Peers

As teens begin to detach from parents and gain independence, it is natural and developmentally appropriate that they gravitate toward peers. At this time in adolescent development, peers take on an outsize importance in helping teens define themselves. "Who I am" is in part defined by who I am with, who accepts me, and who shares my values and interests. As adolescents construct their identity and values, they pick and choose attributes from peers. It's as if they are creating two lists—who they want to be and who they don't want to be: "I want to be kind like Rachel and funny like Jake, but I don't want to be judgmental like Max or a snob like Sydney."

As they attempt to determine who they are and where they fit in, teens seek out new friends and new groups. In this pursuit, it is common for teens to experiment socially, flitting from clique to clique, often with fickle friendships. It's as though they are looking to anchor their sometimes wobbly self-esteem in a peer group, a friend, or a romantic relationship that will make them feel better about themselves. This social experimentation, however, often produces drama and stress, as teens gain and lose friends and fall in and out of favor with various groups. Add to this the tendency to ruminate ("Why did I do that?" "Why did I say that?") and you have a recipe for emotional distress, especially when it comes to matters of the heart.

Teens want to be accepted for their unique self, but at the same time have a strong need for affiliation. Their need to gain and maintain their status in a group makes them susceptible to peer pressure. That peer pressure can be positive, such as when a group of friends studies hard or engages in hobbies or interests together, or negative, such as when a peer group participates in bullying, cuts class, or shows others how to cheat on exams. When peer pressure collides with adolescent tendencies toward impulsiveness and risk taking, it can often result in poor choices, from breaking minor rules at school or ignoring curfew to more serious actions, such as driving recklessly or drinking. When these choices conflict with messages from parents, teens face a stressful dilemma. With a foot in both worlds, teens attempt to please two masters: peers, their source of identity and independence, and parents, whose approval they still very much want and need.

The Virtual World

It's impossible to discuss the world of peers without also discussing the medium through which much peer interaction happens: the virtual world. Although an adolescent's virtual world may include activities such as gaming, the discussion here focuses on social media as the most prominent player in a teen's virtual world.

The virtual world has been a part of adolescent life for quite some time, serving in large part as the lens through which teens perceive the larger world beyond their community. Social media platforms such as TikTok, Instagram, Facebook, X (formerly Twitter), and others have morphed into their own communities, each with its own unique culture. At a time when adolescents are struggling to develop their identities and the world inside their heads is deluged with the voices of parents and peers, the virtual world is omnipresent and a world in which they must participate for their social survival. To fully appreciate the impact of the virtual world on adolescents' development and mental health, we must explore all the roles it can play in their lives, both good and bad.

Social media is a tempting scapegoat for all that ails adolescents, but it's impossible to generalize about its effects on teens. The risks and benefits vary depending on what teens see and do online, the amount of time they spend online, their maturity level, and any preexisting mental health conditions (Mayo Clinic, 2024). For most teens, the virtual world has proven to be both a blessing and a curse.

On the positive side, social media helps teens stay in touch with current friends and connect to new friends with whom they share hobbies, interests, or experiences. Social media can help teens meet their fundamental human needs to connect with others and to belong to a group. That sense of belonging to a community is especially important for kids who feel marginalized, such as LGBTQ+ teens or members of racial, ethnic, or religious minorities. On the negative side, social media can add a layer of anxiety during the already stressful period of adolescence.

The reason is that the virtual world is both lens and a filter, sorting and distorting reality and controlling which messages are received and internalized. As a lens through which teens view the world, it often shows doctored images of perfection and showcases only the best of peers' lives. Given the fragile self-esteem of many adolescents, this facade of perfection often leads to feelings of insecurity. Girls are especially vulnerable because they spend more time on social media than boys, they use more visually oriented platforms like Instagram and TikTok, and they are more inclined to make physical comparisons on those platforms (Haidt, 2024).

As adolescents try to navigate friendships, social media often reduces interaction to the most concrete, black-and-white level—likes and dislikes and the number of "friends" one has. The danger here is if those numbers become the metric by which teens define themselves or their worth. This can lead some teens to devalue their thoughts, values, and competencies: Does something matter if no one "likes" it? As adolescents clumsily try to meet their need for affirmation, social media provides a quick fix, but it is a poor substitute for the genuine connection and support of face-to-face friendships.

The virtual world is also a stage to showcase one's identity and competencies. But the audience is unpredictable—it may affirm, ignore, or ridicule the one in the spotlight—which is how this world can be most harmful to teen mental health. The nature of the medium easily exploits the vulnerabilities of adolescent emotional and social tendencies, such as a lack of impulse control or a penchant for overdramatizing. The instantaneous, full-disclosure quality of social media makes it all too easy to impulsively spill one's most intimate, intense feelings (which adolescents are prone to do). When it comes to responding to someone else's post or sharing a racy picture, there is no impulse delay system, there are no guardrails, and a post may leave a digital trail that can never be erased. It's the virtual equivalent of being naked on a billboard, either emotionally or physically.

In addition to the potential harms of social media, the virtual world presents other risks to teens. The developing adolescent brain is physiologically vulnerable to addiction to both substances and activities (Steinberg, 2014). The combination of an increase in dopamine receptors and typical sensation-seeking behavior makes teens an easy target for smartphone addiction. The device has been programmed to reward sensation seeking with dopamine hits from those "likes" and a 24-7 push of content, without regard to whether the content is harmful.

Although the great majority of teens are not clinically addicted to their phones, checking their phones can easily develop into a bad habit that interferes with face-to-face interaction. In social situations, the smartphone is the great escape, a quick fix for shyness or social awkwardness. At a party and feeling uncomfortable talking to people you don't know? Just get out your phone and scroll aimlessly or text someone. Unfortunately, the more a teen uses their phone to avoid the risk of social interaction, the harder it gets for them to *talk* to people and interact socially.

When teens spend an excessive amount of time with the stimulation of the phone, it can not only interfere with sleep and face-to-face interactions but also rob them of unstructured time for important developmental activities—the introspective time teens need to reflect, discover themselves, and form values.

The World of School

When teens pass through the schoolhouse door, they carry with them the stresses of parental expectations, peer relationships, and their needs for identity and competence. Of all the worlds they live in, school is the place where teens spend the most time, yet traditional middle schools and high schools often do a poor job of meeting their developmental needs and may add stressors of their own.

The way teens experience school often runs counter to what they need. For example, we know teens need social interaction with peers, yet students are often expected to work alone, leaving them with little free time to socialize. We know teens benefit from relationships with caring adults, but content coverage often takes priority over building relationships, leading learning to feel content-rich but relationship-poor. Although teens need to discover and celebrate their uniqueness, conformity is often the norm, and differences may be viewed as weaknesses to fix rather than strengths to be embraced. Developmentally, teens need opportunities to explore their interests and discover their competencies, but the one-size-fits-all learning tasks typically assigned to them prevent that. Finally, although teens need independence in their transition to adulthood, schools often micromanage learning, limit autonomy, and overcontrol students' time and movement.

Conclusion

At the beginning of the 20th century, psychologist G. Stanley Hall (1904) coined the phrase "storm and strife" to describe adolescence. That may be a bit melodramatic, but adolescence is a stressful period of incredible emotional, social, and intellectual change, during which time teens are driven to search for identity, competence, and independence.

When, by the nature of their practices, schools ignore the developmental needs of adolescents, they inadvertently make school more stressful for teens. But what if school didn't have to be this stressful? What if we could change the way teens experience school and simultaneously meet their developmental needs and reduce the stress of adolescence? It is possible, but to provide the nurturing environment that adolescents need will require a paradigm shift. That shift is outlined in Chapter 3.

3

Why We Need a Paradigm Shift

In the traditional paradigm, academics rule and achievement at all costs is the goal. But when school practices focus solely on academic achievement, they crowd out adolescents' important psychological needs, hinder their well-being, and make school more stressful than it needs to be. A shift in school practices is necessary to meet students' developmental needs and reduce their stress.

Prerequisite Understandings About Student Well-Being

Before we can shift school practices to support student well-being, we must gain an understanding of what promotes student well-being, how well-being is related to learning, and the positive or negative effects school practices can have on student well-being. Only then can we appreciate the scope of the paradigm shift that is necessary for schools to improve student well-being.

Student Well-Being Is a Necessary Foundation for Academic Learning

The importance of well-being to learning is most obvious when it is absent. We are all keenly aware of the difficulty students have learning when they are hungry or haven't slept, are unsafe at home, or are being bullied at school. Trauma-informed educational research has made that connection abundantly clear (Keels, 2023). But it is equally true that stress, anxiety, and depression shut down the higher functions of the brain and obstruct students' ability to learn. Without well-being, learning is at the very least compromised, if not impossible. The expression "Maslow before Bloom" reminds us of the importance of student well-being to learning (Hargreaves & Shirley, 2022).

Student Well-Being Is Needs Based

Adolescents have the same psychological needs as adults. Self-determination theory identifies three basic human needs as *autonomy, competence,* and *relatedness*—a feeling of being connected to others (Miles et al., 2022; Stixrud & Johnson, 2018). These three needs appear in many other theories, such as Maslow's hierarchy of needs, Seligman's theory of well-being, Glasser's control theory, and Pink's theory of motivation (Glasser, 1992; Hargreaves & Shirley, 2022; Pink, 2009). But according to many psychologists, this list is incomplete. To be happy, feel fulfilled, and have a sense of well-being, people also need work that has purpose and meaning (Fullan, 2021; Hargreaves & Shirley, 2022; Hari, 2018).

For adolescents, well-being is even more complicated because they are in the process of *becoming.* In addition to the aforementioned basic needs, adolescents have unique developmental needs to discover their identity ("Who am I and what do I value?") and competence ("What am I good at?") (Steinberg, 2017). Thus, the basic needs of autonomy, competence, and relatedness serve double duty as they help advance adolescents' developmental needs and transition to adulthood. Basic and developmental needs operate together to influence adolescent well-being.

Student Well-Being Is Relationship Driven

Connectedness is a basic human need—to feel cared about and part of a community (Stixrud & Johnson, 2018). Connectedness is also necessary for adolescents to meet their developmental needs. They need relationships with both adults and peers to form their views of their own identity and sense of competence (Steiner et al., 2019).

Respectful, reciprocal relationships with adults enhance an adolescent's quest for identity and competence. As Hill and Redding (2021) eloquently put it, young people need *mirrors* (adults who provide affirmation); *windows* (adults who show them what is possible); and *guiding lights* (adults who show them the pathway to their goals). Adults also serve as important trusted figures when adolescents are experiencing emotional or social difficulties and as role models that students emulate as they develop their own identities and value systems.

Peers serve as role models, too. As adolescents construct their identities and values, peers expose them to a variety of personalities, interests, lifestyles, and attitudes that feed into their emerging identities. Peers also help fill the important need for belonging and acceptance. Just as adult relationships provide affirmation, peer friendships provide validation. The drive for that acceptance—that "who I am is OK"—is intense. It's as though adolescents realize that having friends and the approval of a social group helps them create a new social network, which will be necessary for them to thrive in their adult life.

School is the ideal environment to facilitate peer relationships, if students are given the time and opportunity to do so. Peer relationships grow when students work together toward shared goals, either in or out of the classroom, and they benefit from a school climate of community, not hypercompetitiveness. Too much competition interferes with the ability to form meaningful relationships. It's hard to connect with others when you're always competing with them.

Student Well-Being Takes a Village

A lack of connection to others is the enemy of well-being, and it's easy for students to get lost in the shuffle at school, especially if they are academically successful and behaviorally compliant. The quiet, withdrawn student easily falls through the cracks compared with the student whose behavior or academic struggle shouts for attention. Yet each of these students may have mental health challenges. It takes everyone—teachers, staff, parents, and students—to ensure the well-being of all students.

Schools can begin by raising the level of mental health literacy of all adults and students and encouraging everyone to commit to looking out for one another. The village mentality is a collective watchdog approach—"If you see something, say something." The goal is to create a family-like climate of support that makes school a safe place to ask for help. Such support requires new roles for both adults and students within and beyond the school and a multifaceted mental health support system. (This system is described in more detail in Chapter 5.)

What the Paradigm Shift Looks Like

The four prerequisite understandings just discussed are the rationale for a shift away from practices that negatively affect students' well-being and toward practices that enhance students' well-being by meeting their developmental needs. A new wellness paradigm embraces a whole child philosophy that balances academics with wellness while respecting and prioritizing adolescent social, emotional, and physical needs. This paradigm is the foundation of developmentally appropriate educational practice and is driven by what adolescents need to grow into mentally healthy adults. The paradigm is multifaceted and, when implemented, results in a fundamental transformation of school culture, school organization and structures, and the teaching and learning experience.

Over time, as we move toward the wellness paradigm, we develop new norms and we change the culture of the school. That cultural shift is unique to each school and community, as is the pace of its evolution. The wellness paradigm requires a shift in four dimensions of school practice:

How student success is defined, how power is structured, how learning is experienced, and how mental health support is experienced.

How Student Success Is Defined

Student success in the traditional paradigm is defined by the achievement culture, the roots of which were detailed in Chapter 1. In this paradigm, the focus is on the future, with a singular definition of what a successful future looks like: admission to an elite college. Further, many believe that the only way to get there is through a bloated résumé of courses and activities, multiple attempts at the SAT, and applications to numerous top-ranked schools that routinely reject up to 90 percent of their applicants. This paradigm's exemplar of a successful student is one who does it all, with an exhaustive inventory of accomplishments, including a perfect GPA, multiple AP courses, and a long list of sports and activities. By the time they enter their junior year, many students (with the help of their parents) have bought into this paradigm and its fixation on the future, placing value only on courses or experiences that feed the college résumé.

This definition of success is an unattainable goal for many of our students, however. Placing college at the center marginalizes the non-college-bound, those who have not been successful students, those who cannot afford it, or those who simply feel it's not the right path for them. What if this goal is unreachable for a student, or the student believes it is unreachable? Are they then a failure? This intense focus on what happens after high school not only devalues adolescents' present experiences but also disregards their developmental needs, leaving many students feeling disenfranchised.

This version of the achievement culture is more prevalent in affluent communities, and it is not embraced by all students and parents. More widespread is the belief that a college education is the only viable path for future success, even though other postsecondary options, such as military service or training in a trade, may be a better fit for many students. Either way, the message that causes the most stress for adolescents is that their answer to the question "What are your plans after high school?" is the most consequential decision of their life. At a time when their identities are still forming and the decision-making part of their brain is still developing, they are expected to have their lives figured out, with no time to explore and no grace for failure. The pressure is suffocating: "Hurry up and choose your path—this is the rest of your life."

This narrow definition of success creates an artificial sense of scarcity of success in many schools, which sabotages adolescents' need for connectedness and community and breeds a culture of hypercompetitiveness that demeans students' unique accomplishments and talents. The attitude of students in such cultures can be encapsulated in the statements "If you're not the best, you're nothing" and "If everyone gets an A, it doesn't mean anything."

A singular focus on achievement also stifles adolescents' development and exploration of their identity. When identity becomes overly tied to achievement—"I am what I achieve," "I'm only as good as my last grade/performance," or, worst of all, "*All* I am are my achievements"—it's easy for students to feel as though their prospects in life are a stark choice between success or failure. With so much of their future riding on their GPA, an outsize fear grows that every assignment, every test, every course grade is a make-or-break moment with their entire future at stake.

Put it all together and it's easy to see why in the traditional paradigm, especially in affluent communities, both teachers and students describe the school environment as a pressure cooker. Unfortunately, when students are scoring well on standardized tests and being admitted to elite colleges, the belief is often that the pressure-cooker environment is the only way to get to both the elite college and the subsequent successful future (Vatterott, 2019).

The wellness paradigm attempts to break free from the achievement culture, to reshape school culture to focus more on the present than on the future, and to balance academics with wellness. The antidote is threefold. First, it requires us to think carefully about the messages we send to students and parents about success and achievement. What is in the trophy case and what is recognized at awards ceremonies are messages about which competencies are valued. A school can showcase a narrow definition of success limited to academics, sports, or accomplishments that merit scholarships, or it can showcase more diverse interests and accomplishments of students both within and outside school. The latter choice respects a broad range of student identities and competencies, reducing the focus on a narrow path to success.

Second, the wellness paradigm rebrands the postsecondary decision as a way station to each student's future—an exploratory period in life—not as an irreversible destination. We reinforce this view by offering career education that highlights the dignity and value of multiple postsecondary options, such as best-fit colleges, military service, trade schools, or taking a gap year. This shift requires some changes in the way counselors present college and other postsecondary options, reinforcing that all have value and that finding the best fit for each student is what is most important.

Finally, the wellness paradigm prioritizes the development of individual strengths, talents, and interests. A wide range of talents, service projects, acts of altruism, and works of creative expression are valued, encouraged, and celebrated in a school that has shifted its culture this way. Because success has been redefined as personal development, courses and activities are valued for the role they play in helping students meet that goal. This broader concept of success means competition for a few coveted positions decreases and a sense of community grows as students with like interests are drawn to collaborative activities. Because there is no longer only one recognized path to success, students are better able to realize their unique potential.

Figure 3.1 highlights some key differences in how student success is defined in the traditional paradigm versus the wellness paradigm.

How Power Is Structured

In the traditional paradigm, school is a top-down place, with adults holding most of the power. Students are routinely excluded from making decisions or solving problems that affect their school. Rules are created by adults telling students what they can do, when and how they can do it, and where they can go. Those rules often limit basic freedoms like eating, talking, and use of the restroom, restrictions most adults would not tolerate in their work environment. Student behavior and movement are tightly controlled and constantly supervised. The scheduling of time is prescribed down to the minute. This tight control feels especially constricting as adolescents need autonomy to develop independence and competence.

Figure 3.1
How Student Success Is Defined

Traditional Paradigm	Wellness Paradigm
School is a means to an end: elite college and financial success.	School helps students discover their strengths, talents, and interests and form relationships.
There is one path to success: the Ivy League.	There are many paths to success, including best-fit colleges, trade or technical education, apprenticeships, military service, or taking a gap year.
Future success is the primary focus and academic performance is high-stakes, with students' futures and livelihoods hanging in the balance.	Wellness and personal development in the present are the primary focus; postsecondary plans are a way station to the future.
Student identity is defined by numbers (e.g., GPA, number of AP courses taken, and test scores).	Academic performance is just one part of a student's identity, which also encompasses creative talents, interests, altruism, and service to school and community.
The culture is competitive, promoting an artificial sense of scarcity of success. Only a few are on top.	The culture is communal, fostering a sense of belonging. Everyone is in this together, and unique accomplishments are valued.
Courses and activities are valued for feeding the college résumé.	Courses and activities are valued for the role they play in personal development and wellness.

The traditional paradigm reflects distrust of and disrespect for students. Sometimes the rules and restrictions for middle and high school students resemble those for much younger students (Benson, 2019). It's as though the adults' views of student behavior and their resulting rules have been permanently tainted by the actions of a few students who have broken rules in the past.

Becoming an adult should be an exciting venture, yet we stifle that journey with overly restrictive rules and a micromanaged schedule. We tell adolescents to choose their adult path while simultaneously treating them like children, depriving them of the autonomy and freedom they need to grow and develop. Developmentally, it is akin to keeping a toddler in a playpen 24-7 and then wondering why they are not learning to walk.

The power dynamic is present in the traditional classroom as well as in the larger school. It is not uncommon for traditional classrooms to have restrictions about talking, moving, eating, and using the restroom (*Be here in your seat when the bell rings!*). Can students really not be trusted with more freedom? Such traditional methods of classroom management not only compromise adolescent developmental needs for autonomy but are out of sync with how the brain learns: Rules against getting out of one's seat and interacting with other students, for example, run counter to the adolescent brain's needs for movement and to process learning by talking with others (Armstrong, 2016).

In the wellness paradigm, we accept that a rigid hierarchy of power is incompatible with the developmental needs of adolescents. We recognize that to meet their needs for autonomy and competence, we must give them some control over their school experience. They need opportunities for decision making, real-world problem solving, collaboration, and leadership to prepare them for their future (Steinberg, 2017).

In the wellness paradigm, students are treated more as adults are in a workplace, with rules and restrictions limited to what is needed for a safe and effective learning environment (Benson, 2019). In the classroom, brain-friendly practices give students the freedom to take breaks, stand or move, or get a drink when they need to. During the school day, they have some autonomous time, which allows them to connect with friends and feel less rushed. Governance of the school is collaborative, with students given input on decisions that directly affect them, such as master schedule development, course and club offerings, hiring of personnel, and budget allocation. Students operate in leadership roles, make meaningful contributions to school culture and school improvement, and may initiate and manage programs and activities. These practices meet students' needs to have autonomy and develop competence and help them build adult decision-making and problem-solving skills.

Figure 3.2 highlights some key differences in how power is structured in the traditional paradigm versus the wellness paradigm.

Figure 3.2
How Power Is Structured

Traditional Paradigm	Wellness Paradigm
Rules reflect lack of trust; student behavior and movement are constantly supervised.	Rules reflect trust and respect, giving students appropriate adult freedoms.
Rules restrict students' basic physical needs (e.g., movement, eating, restroom visits).	Rules are limited to maintaining a safe and effective learning environment.
Time is tightly prescribed and scheduled to the minute.	Students have some autonomous time and are asked for input on the master schedule.
School governance and school improvement initiatives are directed by adults.	Students play a participatory role in governance and may develop and manage initiatives.
Rules, budget, and hiring are the sole purview of adults.	Students play a role in making decisions about rules, budget, and hiring.

How Learning Is Experienced

The power dynamic in the traditional classroom has real ramifications for learning. In a traditional classroom, the teacher is in charge and learning is tightly prescribed, leaving students with little or no control over the learning tasks they are assigned, the process of learning, how they demonstrate their learning, or when the tasks must be completed. When students have such limited control over their learning, the learning process lacks meaning and often causes them to become passive and disengaged (McTighe & Tucker, 2022). Not only can it be mind-numbing, stressful, and demotivating, but it also leaves secondary students woefully unprepared for college, where they are expected to be more independent learners, to generate and organize their own thinking, and to make decisions about their learning (Vatterott, 2022).

Traditional grading practices are also stress-inducing, limiting the amount of control students have over their grades. Rigid practices such as making all grades permanent, averaging all grades together, and giving one-shot assessments leave students with no options for improving poor performance. For struggling learners, these practices can dampen initiative and make failure a *fait accompli* (Feldman, 2019; Vatterott, 2015). Traditional grading and homework practices tend to reward compliance over learning, often diminishing the teacher-student relationship to a transactional exchange that lacks the emotional support and learning opportunities that students need to improve. These practices define learning merely as a means to an end (complete the work, get that grade!), not as the exciting and meaningful adventure that learning can be.

In the wellness paradigm, learning itself is the focus—not the amount of work produced or number of points accumulated. Students are given more control over the learning process by getting to choose how they will learn and how they will demonstrate their learning. Customizing the learning experience to fit their needs enables students to find meaning in their learning and gives them valuable practice for the self-direction that will be required of them in college and careers. Grading in the wellness paradigm typically incorporates practices used in standards-based grading, such as using homework as ungraded feedback and having multiple opportunities to demonstrate mastery. These practices give students more control over their grades, reduce assessment and grading stress, and result in improved engagement in learning (Armstrong, 2016; Vatterott, 2015).

When we give students more control over their learning and their grades, something profound happens. The teacher-student relationship shifts from a transactional, quid pro quo "Have you completed the required tasks?" exchange to a respectful, supportive "How can I help you reach your learning goal?" dynamic. This change allows for more robust connections between teachers and students that ultimately provide the mental health support that students need (Niemiec & Ryan, 2009).

Figure 3.3 highlights some key differences in how learning is experienced in the traditional paradigm versus the wellness paradigm.

Figure 3.3
How Learning Is Experienced

Traditional Paradigm	Wellness Paradigm
Teaching centers on compliance and controlling students.	Teaching centers on learning and engaging students.
Learning is teacher-prescribed, with little student investment.	Learning is student-driven, meaningful, and joyful; student voice and choice are emphasized.
The learning culture promotes disengagement, passivity, and stress.	The learning culture promotes engagement and competence.
There's a strong focus on quantity of work produced and points accumulated.	There's a strong focus on learning and mastery.
Assessment is an event.	Assessment is a process.
Teacher-student relationships are transactional, with a quid pro quo dynamic.	Teacher-student relationships are collaborative and supportive.
Homework is about compliance.	Homework is about feedback for learning.
Learning is a means to an end.	Learning has value in its own right.

How Mental Health Support Is Experienced

In the traditional paradigm, the approach to student mental health challenges is reactive and similar to emergency room triage—only the sickest are seen as a priority. Student well-being is something of an afterthought, often limited to physical health, behavior, attendance, and, of course, any concerns about abuse or neglect. Sometimes an issue during school hours, such as failing grades or acting out, spills over into the areas of attendance, behavior, or learning and garners the attention of adults as a sign of deeper problems. The typical approach is to "fix" the behavior, much like the behaviorist approach to discipline, without making a more thorough investigation of possible mental health challenges. Only after behavioral fixes have been exhausted is mental health considered. All too often, it takes a more serious problem (such as self-harm, substance abuse, or troubling social media posts) to trigger a mental health intervention and evaluation. Those interventions are typically the responsibility of school administrators and counselors, who often refer students to school psychologists and other mental health professionals outside the school. Those outside referrals are usually reserved for extreme cases (again, only the sickest are seen). This process of referring out stigmatizes those who need help. Because mental health isn't openly and proactively addressed in the traditional paradigm, students often feel that their mental health is not a concern of the school, and that it is something to hide or deny. This lack of attention to student mental health makes it easy for adults to dismiss students' emotional needs as unimportant and can discourage students from seeking help.

In recent years, the traditional paradigm has evolved to include teaching such coping strategies as mindfulness and deep breathing and implementing social-emotional learning. Unfortunately, when it comes to actual mental health challenges, these programs still reflect the approach of fixing behaviors and managing the symptoms of poor mental health without addressing the underlying causes.

Unlike the reactive approach of the traditional paradigm, the wellness paradigm is proactive. We pay attention, we look for warning signs, and we surround students with the support of adults and peers. The wellness paradigm seeks to normalize mental health support and remove the stigma associated with reactive responses. Mental health becomes part of being healthy. Just as meal programs provide breakfast and lunch and nurses treat physical illness, in the wellness paradigm, schools care for students' mental health. The focus shifts from the symptoms of behavior to the underlying student needs and potential causes of stress. Just as we provide physical wellness screenings (such as for vision and hearing), in the wellness paradigm we universally screen all students to assess mental health. This is the first step in a multifaceted mental health support program that includes wellness education for all students and adults, accommodations to reduce school stressors, and partnerships with mental health professionals. (These practices are detailed in Chapter 5.)

Figure 3.4 highlights some key differences in how mental health support is experienced in the traditional paradigm versus the wellness paradigm.

Figure 3.4
How Mental Health Support Is Experienced

Traditional Paradigm	Wellness Paradigm
The approach to mental health is reactive, with an "emergency room/triage" mentality (only the sickest are seen).	The approach to mental health is proactive, with multifaceted mental health screening and support for all students.
Mental health challenges are seen as a psychological disability.	Mental health is seen as a part of overall health.
The focus is on fixing student behavior.	The focus is on understanding and nurturing student needs.
Mental health support is counselor centered.	All adults and students play a role in student mental health and well-being.
Mental health support focuses on how students can cope with stress and handle emotions.	Mental health support focuses on reducing stressors and on education, including mental health literacy, brain research, and lifestyle changes.

Conclusion

The traditional paradigm is not only the antithesis of the whole child philosophy but also developmentally inappropriate for adolescents, and it adds to the inherent stress of this life stage. To address student well-being today, we must first acknowledge how traditional school practices often fail to meet adolescents' developmental needs, deprive them of their need for autonomy, and reinforce the messages of the achievement culture. Then we must go beyond the common interventions of social-emotional learning and stress management to the heart of everyday school practices.

To shift to a wellness paradigm, we must walk the walk of whole child philosophy. That will require us to change school practices to prioritize student needs, redefine student success, and empower students in the classroom. Classroom teachers have an opportunity to enhance adolescent students' well-being, reduce stress, and help them meet their developmental needs for autonomy, belonging, and acceptance. Chapter 4 illustrates how to do so.

4

The Less Stressful Classroom

For adolescents, school is a big part of their life—it is their job, their primary social world, an environment where they spend many of their waking hours. During the school day, most of their time is spent in classrooms, with teachers and peers. And the classroom is the place where educators have the most impact and the greatest chance to reduce students' stress and enhance their well-being.

Adolescents' well-being depends on how well their developmental needs for autonomy, belonging, and acceptance are met. To meet those needs and create a less stressful classroom, teachers need to pay attention to four dimensions of students' classroom experience: relationships, classroom norms and routines, student learning, and grading and homework practices.

Prioritizing Relationships and Building a Sense of Belonging

Research has shown that strong relationships with teachers and peers give students a reason to come to school and to engage in learning. Strong student connections to school are linked to improved mental health and better attendance and grades (Stone, 2024a). A sense of belonging and connection to school has been shown to be a protective factor for adolescent mental health (Steiner et al., 2019).

The need to belong and be accepted is especially important for adolescents who are academically at risk and for students who already feel marginalized because of their racial or ethnic background, religion, primary language, gender identity, or sexual orientation. In surveys, these students were less likely to say they felt connected at school (Stone, 2024b).

What does belonging feel like? The following are some examples I've gathered of what students say makes them feel that they belong to their classroom community:

- I am accepted by the teacher and other students for who I am.
- My teacher and classmates are interested in me.
- My teacher and classmates know things that are important to me.
- My teacher and classmates know something about my life outside school.
- My teacher and classmates notice when I am absent or if I change my appearance.
- I have things in common with the teacher and other students.
- My teacher and classmates remember my name and know how to pronounce it.

A culture of belonging does not just happen—it emerges from a foundation of humanity and caring and from affording everyone dignity. It grows organically when the teacher establishes classwide respect, trust, and shared power. The teacher sets the tone, explicitly models how everyone should treat one another, and monitors that behavior within the group. It is important for the teacher not just to pay lip service to this idea, but also to follow through with their actions. For example, it's great to put an LGBTQ+ "safe space" sticker on your door, but it would be cold comfort if LGBTQ+ students don't believe they are treated with respect by their peers.

Teacher-Student and Student-Student Relationships

New teachers used to be told, "Don't smile until Christmas." Such advice was shorthand for the widespread belief that if you weren't a strict authoritarian, you would lose control of your classroom. Today, most educators understand that a positive teacher-student relationship is essential to learning. Students need to see that the teacher is their advocate and the classroom is a safe space providing a learning experience and peer interactions free from embarrassment and shame.

Before the first day of a new class, most students are a little apprehensive. *Will the teacher be nice or mean? Will I be treated with respect? Will the teacher be overly controlling, or will students have a voice in how the class runs?* On that first day, the teacher communicates (sometimes nonverbally, through facial expressions and body cues) who they are and whether they care about getting to know their students. Relationship building begins immediately, as students form their initial impressions. Teachers can capitalize on that first day by prioritizing getting acquainted with students.

A little teacher self-disclosure goes a long way toward alleviating student concerns. The more teachers reveal about themselves—details like their family, hobbies, and personal history—the more students begin to see them as real people. This sharing also sends a message to students that it is safe to reveal similar details about themselves.

The next step is for the teacher to get to know the students and for students to get to know one another, which can prove challenging. Between the social isolation of the COVID-19 pandemic and the overreliance on virtual relationships, some adolescents need help interacting face-to-face and in groups. When in unfamiliar groups, adolescents often retreat to the safety and comfort of looking at their phones instead of engaging with others. An easy strategy on the first day is conducting a rotating group introduction, where students meet their classmates and share a few facts about themselves. Here's a structured strategy I used to help my undergraduates get acquainted on the first day of class:

First, each student completes a notecard listing three facts about themselves or things that are important to them that they are comfortable sharing with other students and the teacher. Some students may list hobbies, pets, favorite television shows, or favorite sports teams, while others may share that their faith or family is important to them or present facts about their cultural or ethnic background. Before the teacher sees the notecards, the students will share them with other students.

The teacher has a stack of different-colored cards with pictures of various symbols, such as a car, a house, a boat, and a fish (playing cards could also be used). Each color set includes one of each symbol card (e.g., the green set includes a car card, a house card, and so on). Each student chooses a random card from the whole stack of cards, which places them in both a color group and a symbol group. Students meet first with their color group and share their three facts. Then students switch to their symbol group and share their facts again.

The teacher then collects the students' notecards and goes through them, making a quick verbal connection to each student as the class listens: "Brad, I see you collect vinyl; how cool," and "Ashley, I'm a dog lover, too!"

This activity not only introduces each student to the class but also allows for a one-on-one connection with the teacher. Everyone now knows something about everyone else, and usually they learn more about their teacher, too. They also get to see that the teacher is interested in who they are, is searching for common ground, and is treating them respectfully.

Learning students' names and how to pronounce them correctly should be the teacher's top priority in the first week with a new group. Some teachers have students wear name tags for a few days, which helps both teachers and classmates learn student names. It is helpful for students to spend time working in small groups the first few days, with the teacher switching up the group combinations so students get to work with all their classmates. One teacher actually gives students a quiz (ungraded, of course) of student names at the end of the first week (Vatterott, 2007). Teachers can also take class time to test themselves on student names, seeking feedback on accuracy and pronunciation. Students might also share the origins or meaning of their names.

Some teachers ask students to greet one another or have a quick conversation before class begins. Instructionally, the classroom community benefits from whole-group discussions, partner work, and teacher-chosen groups that require students to work with lots of different classmates. Eventually, students get comfortable with their peers and trust that this is a safe place to learn.

Developing a sense of belonging is not a one-and-done activity. The teacher makes it happen on a daily basis by taking a little time for a casual conversation in the hallway, at lunch, or at the beginning of class. When a researcher friend of mine asked students, "How do you know teachers care?" one response was, "They talk to you when they don't have to." Striking up a conversation could be as simple as asking about a student's weekend or just how things are going. Such inquiries show that the teacher is interested in students' lives outside class and considers student well-being to be as important as learning.

When teachers know something about their students' lives outside the classroom (and vice versa), it makes it easier for students to believe their teacher actually cares about them as people. It's hard for students to believe a teacher cares about them when the teacher doesn't know anything about them.

A teacher need only know a few things about students to be able to connect to them personally. Knowing things like who plays which sports, who is in the school play, and who is a fan of a particular sports team goes a long way toward building connection. One middle school social studies teacher shared the following:

> One kid, he's a White Sox fan. I don't even like the White Sox, but I'll check the sports page to see what they did, and I'll say something to him walking in the door. "The Sox looked terrible last night." If I say it to him once in three weeks, he knows that I know he's a White Sox fan, and it makes him feel special. (Vatterott, 2007, p. 86)

There's one group of students that requires a little extra help with belonging. Students who are frequently absent, are usually disengaged, or seem to have little interaction with their classmates often feel unseen.

As Brooks (2023) put it, "No crueler punishment can be devised than to *not* see someone, to render them unimportant or invisible.... To do that is to say: You don't matter. You don't exist" (p. 9). These are the students teachers often fail to develop a relationship with because, well, it's just harder. These students often make it so easy for the teacher and students to ignore them. Yet these are the students most in need of connection with a caring adult. A welcoming one-on-one conversation—"Good to see you, glad you're back!"—before class that can be overheard by others helps them feel seen. Sometimes teachers will ask another particularly helpful student to tell the absent student what they missed. The teacher can give these students a little extra attention in the learning process by asking them questions and checking on their progress on tasks or by placing them with a supportive student group.

It's hard for students to build a relationship with the teacher when they have no voice in the relationship or in any aspect of how the classroom runs. The next dimension of students' classroom experience to address is giving students input into classroom rules and routines.

Developing Classroom Norms and Routines

Giving students a voice in classroom procedures seems risky to many teachers. After all, from our teacher preparation programs to our first jobs as teachers, the mantra "Control your classroom" has been drilled into our heads. No wonder teachers are hesitant to give up control.

Most of us can agree that the classroom environment should be safe and orderly; the problem is that the recommended *method* of achieving that controlled environment is often the use of rewards and punishments. Inherent in the carrot-and-stick classroom management method is the assumption that students cannot be trusted to manage their own behavior. But students are not lab rats, capable only of focusing on rewards and punishments—they are complex human beings with needs for acceptance and belonging. They are intrinsically motivated to connect with others and to fit into their social group (Vatterott, 2007).

When we are focused solely on controlling behavior, we lose sight of adolescents' developmental needs, especially their desire for autonomy. When we tell adolescents to follow rules they have no say in—especially when they deem the rules unreasonable—we risk provoking an "us-against-them" mentality in students that prioritizes peer acceptance over rule-following at a time in their lives when peers can be a more powerful influence than adults.

Teacher-made rules that neglect or even go against developmental needs can interfere with learning and cause problems that could easily be avoided by allowing students' input and respecting their needs.

Research has taught us much about the influence of physical needs on the brain's ability to learn. For example, to remain active, the brain needs the body to move every 20 minutes or so (Jensen, 2000). Students who are allowed even short stand-up breaks (i.e., breaks to stand or move when needed) are more attentive and less stressed. Students also benefit from having options in their physical working positions, such as being able to use standing desks, sit in comfortable chairs, or even stretch out on the floor. Middle school students, with their rapidly growing (and sometimes awkward) bodies, especially appreciate freedom of movement and choices in working positions.

Brain research also tells us that the learning brain is quickly dehydrated, and simply giving students access to water has been shown to reduce stress hormones and improve learning (Jensen, 2000). For some students, especially those in the growth cycles of puberty, hunger can also be a distraction, so allowing students to snack when needed (while limiting messiness and distraction to others) can reduce stress.

Problems arise when physical needs are not met: Students can't pay attention when they need to move for a minute, are hungry or thirsty, or need to use the restroom. Physical needs come first and override learning (remember: Maslow before Bloom!).

When we involve students in crafting norms and routines, their physical, psychological, and developmental needs can be met, their stress can be reduced, and class can run more smoothly. The following sections discuss how to incorporate student voice in developing norms and routines. Although both norms and routines outline expectations of students and the teacher (Anderson, 2021), they serve distinct roles.

Working with Students to Create Classroom Norms

Norms answer the questions *What is the optimal learning environment? What do students need to be able to learn?* and *How should we treat one another?*

Collaboratively created norms do leave room for some teacher nonnegotiables. First, of course, are schoolwide regulations that teachers must follow, such as rules about cell phones. But some nonnegotiables are norms that the individual teacher needs to feel comfortable and to remain focused. Just as students will reveal what they need to learn, teachers should explain what they need to teach. For instance, a teacher might say, "I need people to raise their hand to talk during a discussion. When people shout out remarks, I find it hard to maintain my train of thought."

Here are some other possible teacher nonnegotiables:

- We treat everyone with respect.
- We don't interrupt or talk over others in a discussion.
- We help each other with learning, but we don't do other people's work for them.
- We work with everyone, even people we may not like.

The teacher may share these with the class ahead of students creating norms, or simply wait and see if the same norms emerge from the student discussions.

The teacher begins the process by delivering a series of open-ended prompts to get students thinking about what they need to learn and feel comfortable. The teacher can ask students to first reflect on the prompts individually in a freewrite. This ensures that the quieter, shyer students' input is included. The following are some possible examples:

- "I feel comfortable in a classroom where _____."
- "In this classroom, I want to be able to _____."
- "In order for me to learn in this classroom, I need _____."
- "I want other people in the classroom to _____."

Then the process for creating norms moves to small-group discussions using web charts or sticky notes. All students' responses should be recorded. Then the teacher can ask the groups to consolidate their lists of specifics into broader norms. Another option is for each group to share its list with the entire class and then work together as a class to consolidate the norms. For instance, norms such as "Use polite language" and "Don't bother someone while they are working" could be consolidated into "Respect others." There's no "right" number of norms to arrive at; one middle school classroom I visited had just two norms: "Respect others" and "Respect property." Anderson (2021) suggests that teachers and students keep playing with the wording until the class reaches consensus, and then post the norms where they are easy to see.

Working with Students to Define Classroom Routines

If norms lay out guidelines for teachers and students to follow, routines outline the way things are done to make learning go more smoothly and the class in general run more efficiently. Like norms, routines benefit from student input, and here, too, the teacher will have nonnegotiables, some of which may stem from school rules (such as those about the use of cell phones and laptops).

Routines differ for different subjects; an art class will need different routines from a math class or a writing class. Routines also vary for different activities within the same class, such as labs, groupwork, and independent work within a science class. The teacher may invite student input on routines involving beginning and ending the class, returning to class after an absence, participating in group discussions, and working in small groups. If the teacher is comfortable and not bound by schoolwide rules, they may allow student input into what have traditionally been restrictive practices, such as the following:

- When and how to leave the classroom to use the restroom
- When it's OK to talk to other students
- When it's OK to move or take a stand-up break
- When it's OK to eat a snack or drink water

As teachers work collaboratively with students to create rules and procedures, it is important for them to respect students' input and carefully weigh their ideas. For instance, if students say they want to be able to move more, are you able to accommodate that? It's disingenuous to ask for input that you will not consider. If you are not prepared to let students snack in class, for example, you should make it a teacher nonnegotiable upfront and explain your rationale to students.

The Value of Collaboration

It may seem counterintuitive that teachers could actually have more control by giving students more autonomy and voice—but control is not a zero-sum game. Giving students voice does not diminish the teacher's power. By giving students some power, teachers actually gain more control. When students' developmental and physical needs are met, their engagement and learning improve and the class runs more smoothly.

One of the benefits of involving students in setting norms and routines is that quite often students themselves enforce the rules. Students will actually tell their classmates, "Hey, that's not being respectful," or "We don't interfere with other students' learning."

Allowing students input in no way negates the normal structure and limits necessary in any classroom. Many teachers fear that once students are given some power, the privilege can never be revoked. But the classroom does not become a true democracy—the teacher has to function as the adult in the room and always retains veto power.

As classroom community evolves, it's a good idea to periodically revisit norms and routines to assess how well they are working. Class meetings can accomplish this task, and they also give teachers the chance to ask students how things are going and if there are norms or routines the class needs to rethink or add. Many teachers hold class meetings once a month, but either students or the teacher should be able to request a class meeting if they see a need for one. Students can do so anonymously by way of a suggestion box.

The more autonomy and voice students have in the classroom, the better the teacher-student relationship becomes, the more cooperation and engagement teachers see, and the fewer discipline problems teachers have. Inviting student voice helps us create the optimal learning environment. When we free students to get their needs met, we make it possible for them to focus on learning.

Giving Students a Voice in Their Learning

Allowing students to have autonomy in their learning is just as essential as giving them a voice in classroom norms and routines. What do adolescents need from learning? They need

- To feel safe enough to take academic risks.
- To get feedback about their learning that will lead them to mastery.
- To experience mastery so that they feel competent and confident as learners.
- To believe that their work is meaningful and purposeful, and that the tasks are respectful, engaging, and worthy of their time.
- To be able to express their individuality in their work.

When it is structured properly and gives students sufficient autonomy, learning can meet these needs.

"School Is Boring": The Engagement Problem

Engagement is important to student well-being: Engaged students are more likely to show up and do well in school and more likely to be hopeful about their future (Peetz, 2024). But at the middle and high school levels, we have an engagement problem. A large national study (Calderon & Yu, 2016) shows that student engagement in school steadily declines from 5th to 12th grade. The number of students who are engaged or enthusiastic about school falls from 74 percent in 5th grade to 34 percent in 12th grade. By 10th grade, one-third of students reported that they were not engaged with school, while another one-third of students reported that they were actively *disengaged*.

What accounts for the decreasing engagement? The stage of adolescence itself is partly the cause. Psychologists point to the developmental need for autonomy, observing that autonomy in the classroom is the key to unlocking engagement in high school but that many secondary classrooms offer students little, if any, autonomy (Hafen et al., 2012).

When you ask a high school student how they feel about school, the answer you are most likely to get is "It's boring." What's boring is the lack of control students have in the traditional, teacher-centered classroom. At a time when adolescents have a strong need for autonomy, teacher-directed learning offers them little opportunity: The teacher makes all decisions about learning, with step-by-step instructions on what to do and how to do it. Kittle and Gallagher (2020) aptly label this "helicopter teaching." In short, learning is often overdirected and overprescribed.

Educators' tendency to overdirect comes from the best intentions—after all, teachers know the learning goals we want students to reach, we are familiar with the content, and we are confident we know how to get students to the goals. So we assign the same task to the whole class, expect all students to comply, and *voilà!* Learning occurs . . . except when it doesn't (Vatterott, 2018). What we often fail to realize is that our methods are not infallible and may not work for all students.

Beyond feeling a lack of autonomy, many students also don't see the relevance of what they are learning and its connection to the real world or to their lives. Students just won't care much about tasks they had no voice in designing and that have little personal relevance to them.

A lack of autonomy and relevance promotes passivity and disengagement and leads to student stress and apathy (McTighe & Tucker, 2022). Teachers often explain away apathetic students with a dismissive "They just don't care," giving little thought to how they could change that by giving students more input into the learning process. When we control everything about the learning process, we can wind up with students who are disengaged or, worse, misbehaving out of boredom or resentment about their lack of power. Then we wind up policing behavior when we would rather be focusing on learning.

Student apathy and disengagement are dangerous. They put students at risk not only for academic failure but also for tuning out, acting out, and chronic absenteeism, which lead to further disconnection from school and fewer options to meet their needs for competence and connection. And once students have reached this degree of disengagement, the task to engage them becomes that much more difficult.

Although many teachers do their best to make content relevant, granting students autonomy in learning goes further by giving them the freedom to find relevance and meaning in their learning and to connect content to something they know or care about. As one teacher said, "I've never heard of a student not doing *his* work. It's *our* work he's not doing" (Vatterott, 2018).

To improve student engagement and reduce stress, any amount of autonomy in learning is helpful. Autonomy = higher engagement = less stress. But how do we actually go about granting students autonomy in their learning? We begin by shifting our focus from what *we* can do to what *students* can do.

Allowing Students Autonomy in Learning

For teachers who are accustomed to making all the decisions about learning, the idea of giving students autonomy can be downright scary. After all, teachers are responsible for student performance on standards. The pressure to ensure students do well on standardized tests is high, and it often freezes teachers in their methods and makes them afraid to try anything new. Some are white-knuckling it with their instructional strategies in an almost superstitious way, scared that if they change anything it will all fall apart. If students are doing well on standardized tests, it's tempting to rationalize that "If it ain't broke, don't fix it." But the key indicator should be engagement. If engaging students is a struggle and they seem perennially apathetic, then *isn't* it broke? We assume they are doing well on standardized tests *because* of the way we are teaching them—but what if they are doing well *in spite* of the way we are teaching them?

Student autonomy in learning does not mean abandoning teacher-directed learning altogether and simply turning the curriculum over to students. Whatever autonomy we allow students, it is ours to give and, if necessary, ours to take away. Teachers who have allowed students autonomy have learned that, counterintuitively, it gives the teacher a sense of control, as *they* are the ones allowing the choice and freedom. The teacher retains control of the curriculum, but they mediate the curriculum using student autonomy to better engage students.

Most teachers who want to increase student autonomy in learning begin with a single activity or lesson and then reflect on how it worked and how well it went. They also move slowly in terms of the *amount* of autonomy they give students. An easy way to think about it is that we are moving from students having choices, to students having input, to students designing their own learning.

What Student Autonomy in Learning Looks Like

To understand the options for student autonomy, it is helpful to think of four planned components of learning: the learning *goal,* the *content* of the learning, the *process* by which the learning will occur, and the *product* or *method of assessment* showing that the learning goal has been met, be it a traditional assessment (such as a test) or a product or performance created by the student. Ideally, the teacher plans using backward design: The learning goal comes first, and the content, process, and product or method of assessment are designed in service of that goal. Student autonomy may be incorporated in any of these four components, or in any combination of the four.

The learning goal component has the least room for student autonomy, since it is usually mandated by standards, but in student-directed learning environments, students may determine the goal either by themselves or in collaboration with the teacher. The teacher can almost always give students a choice in the content they learn toward the learning goal, how they reach that learning goal, and how they demonstrate that they met the goal. It may be helpful to view autonomy in learning on a broad continuum from totally teacher-directed to mostly student-directed to understand the options that are available to teachers and students (see Figure 4.1).

In Frederick County Public Schools in Virginia, a committee of teachers who were already allowing student autonomy in learning created their own continuum (see Figure 4.2) to help other teachers in the district implement student autonomy in their classrooms. The committee mentored their colleagues by sharing what worked for them and helped those colleagues reflect on lessons they were designing. Their continuum includes student-selected options for learning environment and assessment, such as giving students the freedom to learn alone or with a partner or group.

These continuums are only templates to guide teacher and student creativity. Student autonomy in content, process, and product can fall on

Figure 4.1
Continuum of Student Autonomy in Learning

	Teacher-Directed Learning (no student choice)	Teacher-Centered Learning (managed student choice)	Student-Centered Learning	Student-Directed Learning
Student Autonomy	No student autonomy	Limited student autonomy	Some student autonomy	Lots of student autonomy
Learning Goal	Teacher determines learning goal.	Teacher determines learning goal.	Teacher determines learning goal.	Students determine learning goal, or teacher and students detemine goal collaboratively.
Content, Process, and Product	Teacher chooses content, process, and product.	Teacher designs some process or product options for students to choose from.	Teacher and students make collaborative decisions about content, process, and/or product.	Students choose process and product and, sometimes, content.

different spots on the continuum depending on what makes sense for a given lesson or activity. For instance, for one lesson, the process might be teacher-centered and the product student-centered. Another lesson might offer teacher-managed choices for the learning process but invite student-designed products to demonstrate learning. There are many

60   The Teens Are Not Alright

Figure 4.2
The Frederick County School District Continuum of Teaching and Learning

Inspire
Continuum of Teaching and Learning

Social-Emotional Culture:
A Culture of Connections
Supportive Environment
Growth Mindset
Building Relationships

Frederick County Public Schools

Student Directed

Plan to Design

Content

Student Determines Focus
- Pacing of standards (SOLs)
- Topics of learning

Student & Teacher Determine Focus
- Pacing of standards (SOLs)
- Topics of learning

Teacher Determines Focus
- Pacing of standards (SOLs)
- Topics of learning

Design and Map

Student
- Sets learning goals
- Plans course of research
- Identifies learning process and product

Student & Teacher
- Collaborate on objectives
- Collaborate on lesson structure

Teacher
- Plans objectives
- Writes lessons
- Paces curricula

Teacher Directed

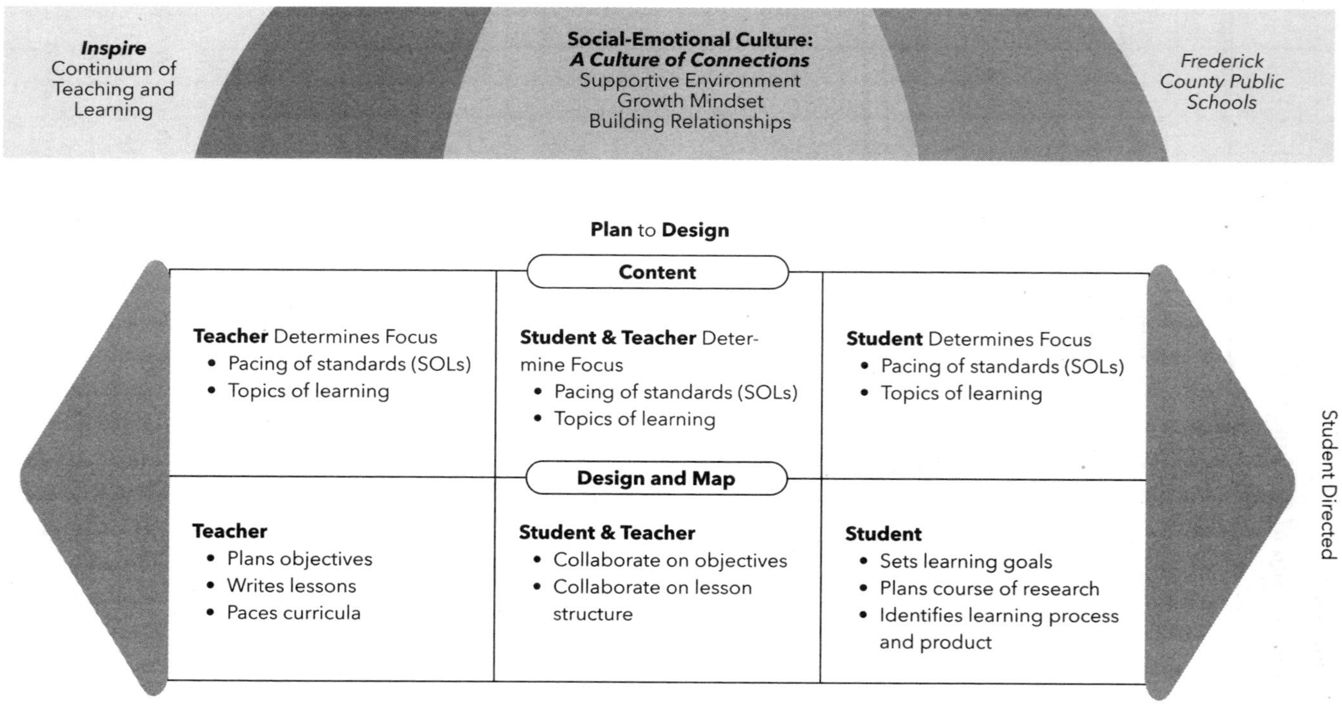

The Less Stressful Classroom 61

Teacher Directed ⇅ **Student Directed**

Teach to Facilitate

Learning Environment

Teacher Chooses
- Seating
- Grouping
- Workspace
- Lighting & sound
- Materials
- Resources

Collaboratively Determine
- Seating
- Grouping
- Workspace
- Lighting & sound
- Materials
- Resources

Student Chooses
- Seating
- Grouping
- Workspace
- Lighting & sound
- Materials
- Resources

Learning Experience

Teacher Centered
- Direct instruction
- Explicit instruction

Collaboratively Centered
- Stations
- Groupwork
- Choice board
- Discussion protocols

Student Centered
- Research
- Passion choice
- Inquiry
- Product creation

Assess to Reflect

Product

Teacher Designs
- Assessment
- Task assignment
- Scoring device

Student & Teacher Design
- Assessment
- Task assignment
- Scoring device

Student Designs
- Assessment
- Task assignment
- Scoring device

Reflection*

Teacher Develops
- A reflection on learning process & goals

Student & Teacher Develop
- A reflection on learning process & goals

Student Develops
- A reflection on learning process & goals

---

* While this continuum indicates Reflection occurs in Assess to Reflect, it is understood that reflection occurs throughout the teaching and learning process; reflection can happen at any point in this continuum.

Finalized July 2023

Source: Courtesy of Frederick County Public Schools. Copyright 2023 Frederick County Public Schools. Printed with permission.

possible combinations of teacher-directed, teacher-centered, student-centered, and student-directed experiences in any unit of study, and student autonomy may vary from day to day or by assignment. Let's take a deeper look at the four categories.

Teacher-directed learning. At the most traditional end of the continuum, all students have the same learning experience. The teacher sets the learning goal and content, determines the one-size-fits-all learning task (process), and designs one product or method of assessment.

Teacher-centered learning. A first step toward student autonomy is to allow some student choice in at least one of these areas. The students may be allowed to choose from two or three teacher-designed learning tasks, such as using videos, selected readings, or various websites as their sources for an exercise. The teacher may also offer choices in the product that demonstrates student learning, such as writing a paper, making a presentation, or crafting a poster. When offering a choice of products, the teacher must make sure that all options demonstrate the same level of learning. Can a poster demonstrate mastery of the same goals as a research paper? A carefully designed rubric should ensure that. In one 7th grade science class, students could choose to make a calendar or a mobile to demonstrate their understanding of the phases of the moon, but both choices were evaluated using the same rubric with the same goals (Vatterott, 2015). When teachers offer choices in teacher-centered learning, the student has a degree of autonomy, but only within the choices that the teacher has created and allows. A helpful resource for creating student choices is Mike Anderson's book *Learning to Choose, Choosing to Learn: The Key to Student Motivation and Achievement* (2016).

Student-centered learning. Student-centered learning goes beyond teacher-managed choices to letting students create their own choices, enabling them to express their individuality in their work. Students may meet learning goals by choosing their own unique content, process, or product, or any combination of the three. Teachers often work collaboratively with students to co-create student-centered learning experiences. Here are some examples of what this could look like in each of the four components of learning:

- *Learning goal:* Teachers begin by sharing the learning goal with students, explained or written as a student-friendly learning target. Then they can ask for input on ways to reach the goal.
- *Content:* With a learning goal of identifying imagery, metaphors, or rhyme schemes in poetry, students have the freedom to choose any poem they wish.
- *Process:* With a learning goal of learning how to speak a foreign language, students choose the process that works for their learning preference, such as using a language app or a written phonetic guide to pronunciation.
- *Product:* With a learning goal of understanding the causes and effects of the Boston Tea Party, students design products as diverse as flowcharts, role-plays, or board games to demonstrate their learning. As with teacher-managed choices, a common rubric for all student-designed products ensures that each meets the same rigorous requirements.

Student-directed learning. On the far-right side of the continuum is what is typically labeled *student-directed learning,* sometimes called *personalized learning.* Student-directed learning gives the student significant autonomy in the learning process, to a degree that many teachers may not be comfortable with. Many teachers save student-directed learning for times when student engagement wanes, such as before winter break or near the end of the school year.

Following are three common types of student-directed learning.

1. *Culminating projects* or *capstone experiences* enable students to demonstrate multiple learning goals, typically at the end of a unit or course, usually through a formal presentation, performance, or project (Kallick & Zmuda, 2017). For instance, students might demonstrate their knowledge of force and motion by designing a carnival ride or through a demonstration of matchbox cars and ramps. Students could demonstrate their knowledge of polygons, proportions, and scale drawings by designing a building, or their knowledge of slope by designing parts of a golf course. Each student may be required to demonstrate the same goals, or the

teacher may work with students individually to determine which goals they should work toward based on their areas of need. For instance, toward the end of the semester, one teacher asked her students to pick their three weakest learning targets. Then she worked with them to design independent projects to deepen their understanding (Vatterott, 2015).

2. *Genius hour projects* (also called *passion projects*) are totally student-directed. Typically, students are given a regular block of time to learn more about something that they are curious about or that excites or inspires them (Vatterott, 2018). In this type of student-directed learning, the student sets their own learning goal and designs the learning process and the product to demonstrate their learning. If their goals seem too simple, are too broad or narrow, or lack a connection to the course, the teacher always has the power to revise or veto them. The teacher's role is to guide students to deeper learning or to a more rigorous or more comprehensive plan. In one 7th grade language arts class, students spent one hour a week in class over the course of the school year on their genius projects (with monthly goals and teacher feedback) and presented their projects to parents and community members at a Genius Hour Showcase in May. Topics ranged from animal rights to effects of the media and how the brain learns (Vatterott, 2018).

3. *Short student-directed learning activities* can be used to stimulate interest in a new topic or to allow students to reflect on their learning. One method is to present students with a question such as "Why was the Vietnam War controversial?" or "Why are covalent bonds important?" and invite students to research the question by reading anything they like. They then answer the question and reflect on the results by answering one of a series of prompts, relating their research to other concepts in the unit. A similar activity could be used at the end of a unit to allow students to learn more about something that interested them (Vatterott, 2018).

Here's what student-directed learning looks like when it is embedded in a course. At Basehor-Linwood High School in Basehor, Kansas, Innovation Academy is a cross-curricular course option that meets student requirements for ELA and social studies. Each grade level, from 9 through 12, has its own section of the course. Students work in small teams to conceive, design, plan, and implement a project that meets a community need. For example, one team designed a park and playground and submitted its plan to the city for approval. The students follow a design thinking process that is scaffolded by the teachers to meet many of the ELA and social studies standards for their grade level. The scaffolding includes identifying a problem and a client, determining customer needs and wants, creating a prototype, and designing a website.

Teacher-student interaction in the Innovation Academy classroom looks very different from that in a traditional classroom. Teacher-led direct instruction is limited mostly to short minilessons delivered to the whole class about the part of the project that students are working on. Students spend the bulk of the time working independently or in groups with the teacher monitoring their progress, periodically checking in and answering each group's questions, serving more as a consultant than as a teacher.

Where the Magic Happens

Teachers often feel great passion for the content they teach and enjoy sharing it with their students. If they are lucky, that enthusiasm is contagious, and their students catch it. When students have some control over what they learn and how they learn it, they develop a personal relationship with the content, much like the teacher does, and they get excited about their learning. That is where the magic happens.

Suddenly, learning becomes not just a means to an end (a grade), but satisfying in its own right—meaningful, purposeful, and possibly even joyful! When teachers see the enthusiasm and joy students experience as they get excited about their learning, teachers get excited, too. Isn't that why we became teachers—to watch students find joy in learning?

Further, teachers who have allowed students to direct their own learning often discover things about their students that they didn't know before. Getting to know their students better also improves their connections with parents. They see untapped leadership abilities in students that they never would have suspected, and talents they never knew about.

They see formerly struggling students successfully learning and feeling better about themselves.

Rethinking Grading and Homework Practices

If we are concerned about student stress, and if we have decided to give students a degree of autonomy in their learning, does it follow that traditional practices such as grading, homework, and use of time should also change? The answer is that they don't have to—but they should.

Giving students autonomy in how they learn and show their learning is an important step in meeting adolescent developmental needs and reducing stress, but it only goes so far. Adolescents' identity is tied to their feelings of competence—the perception of how good they are at doing the job of school. Many traditional grading practices make it easy to feel incompetent at a time when there is so much pressure to get good grades. High achievers and perfectionists often have too much of their identity tied up in getting good grades. Anything less than an *A* may feel like failure to them, which ramps up their stress. And struggling students who don't do well with traditional grading can easily adopt the fixed mindset that "I'm just not smart." That mindset gets integrated into their identity as well, making them feel worse about themselves.

When high school students were asked to rate their top sources of stress, grades, tests, and other assessments topped the list, with overall workload and homework a close second (Challenge Success & NBC News, 2021). Those results remained relatively consistent before and during the pandemic. This is not surprising given the fact that traditional assessment and grading practices leave students with limited control over their grades.

How to Make Grades Less Stressful

We can neutralize much of the stressful effect of traditional grading by putting in place the following student-friendly practices.

Grade less and give more ungraded feedback. When everything is graded—including first attempts and mistakes made while still learning—grades become a stressful endeavor for students. One bad grade can drive down a student's average and seal their fate, GPA-wise. A low grade is the gift that keeps on giving... stress.

Traditional grading practices are set up so that there will be a limited number of high grades sheerly by virtue of student diversity. Those high grades are much more accessible to students who are quick studies, fast processors, and strong test takers. The artificial scarcity of high grades sets up competition, which compromises the ability of students to connect with one another and interferes with their need for belonging and peer acceptance.

But by grading less and providing more ungraded feedback on assignments, teachers can reinforce that learning is not an error-free process and that mistakes are a normal and necessary part of that process. Ideally, ungraded feedback would be a one-on-one conversation between teacher and student. Unlike written feedback, a face-to-face conversation makes it easy for the student to ask questions about the feedback in real time. For some long-term projects, such as research papers, taking time in class to give students one-on-one feedback is actually more efficient, is more personal, and feeds the teacher-student relationship. That said, to find class time to have the one-on-one requires the teacher to limit direct instruction and incorporate activity-based learning. Ungraded feedback could also take the form of whole-class discussion, self-assessment, or peer evaluation. Here's how Wiliam (2007) describes one peer evaluation strategy:

> Before students can turn in an assignment, they must trade papers with a peer. Each student then completes a "pre-flight checklist" by comparing the peer's document against a list of required elements. For example, the pre-flight checklist for a lab report might require, among other things, a title, a date, diagrams drawn in pencil and labeled, and results that are clearly separated from conclusions. Only when the peer has signed off on the checklist can the work be turned in to the teacher. (p. 194)

No-count practice tests are also useful as feedback. Students can get feedback from practice tests by scoring their own papers and discussing their mistakes and misunderstandings in small groups or as a class. The scores are used strictly as feedback to the student and need not be recorded. If teachers wish to record practice test scores or other formative feedback, the score should be given zero weight in the gradebook. As a colleague of mine (who was also a coach) once said, "If we have a bad practice, we don't show up at the game with negative 10 points on the scoreboard."

Change the structure and conditions of in-class assessments. One-shot tests and quizzes make assessment a high-stakes game. The test is at 10:00 a.m. on Tuesday for everyone—whether a student is ready or not. Too bad if a student is having a bad day, did not study in the most efficient way, or anticipated multiple-choice but got essay questions. Too bad, too, if the assessment is time-based and some learners have slower working speeds than others: Everyone gets the same time to complete the test. It's no wonder some students have test anxiety!

There are some low-lift ways teachers can ease this anxiety. If some students struggle to complete a test in the time allotted, teachers might consider shortening the test, breaking up longer tests into two or three shorter tests given over consecutive days, or giving shorter quizzes more frequently. The teacher might also survey students for readiness prior to an assessment and, if many of them indicate they are not ready, the teacher could give additional formative assessments and feedback. Postponing an assessment for a few days not only gives students more time for learning but also often results in better student performance and less stress.

Provide multiple opportunities to demonstrate mastery. Thinking of a test as performance on demand, with no do-overs, is enough to ramp up anyone's stress level. To reduce assessment stress, it is important to consider assessment as a process rather than an event. When we shift our mindset from "getting it right the first time" to simply "getting it right," we not only enable students to experience competence, but we also reduce competition among students and allow our community of learners to develop, with everyone in pursuit of a common goal.

Offering retakes on assessments and revisions on assignments enables students to continue to learn and gives a chance of redemption for a poor first performance. There are caveats, however. When redoing assignments, students need to receive and follow specific feedback before submitting their revision. Similarly, assessment retakes require remediation. Allowing retakes with no evidence that additional learning has occurred is frustrating, time-consuming, and stressful for both students and teacher. Prior to retaking an assessment, students should first complete some form of remediation, such as watching and responding to a video, completing additional practice, meeting with the teacher for reteaching, or proposing their own method based on a self-assessment. Only then should students be eligible for a retake. Once the student has improved their performance, new information should *replace* the old information as opposed to being averaged with the first grade, as we assume the most recent evidence of learning is the most accurate. (For more ideas about grading, see *Rethinking Grading: Meaningful Assessment for Standards-Based Learning* [Vatterott, 2015].)

Homework Stressors and What to Do Instead

Homework ranks close behind assessment as a major stressor for students. There are three aspects of homework practices that cause stress: grades, tasks, and time, all of which could be made less stressful by giving students more autonomy and, dare I say, a bit of grace.

Homework grades. During the last several years, a consensus has emerged among assessment experts that homework is formative assessment, should be used as ungraded feedback, and should not be part of the course grade. When homework counts in the grade, it becomes an equity issue, penalizing students who are unable to complete work at home. It is equally problematic to count homework in the grade when we are unsure of who actually completed the homework or how much "help" students received from parents, tutors, or AI tools. When teachers stop counting homework in the grade, they take the heat off stressed-out students and put them in control of their learning. Contrary to the myth that if homework is ungraded "they just won't do it," not grading homework gives students the autonomy to determine what they need to do to reach mastery and to complete only those tasks they actually need to do.

For teachers who feel obligated to count homework in the grade, it's best to limit its weight to 5–10 percent of the total grade, so the grade is a more accurate reflection of student learning. Limiting the weight of homework both minimizes the negative impact of incomplete homework on the grade and blunts the potential of homework completion to obscure poor performance on assessments and other learning tasks. Assessment retakes and revisions of other student work become especially important when homework is not included in the grade.

Not grading homework reduces stress for teachers, too—they spend less time marking and recording homework and chasing missing homework, and more time monitoring student learning and giving ungraded feedback.

Homework tasks. Traditionally, teachers have designed one-size-fits-all homework tasks based on the learning goal they want students to reach. Because not all learners benefit from the same task, this can cause stress for many students. Students who have already mastered the goal may find the homework tedious and unnecessary, while struggling learners may not be able to complete the task at all, leading to stress and frustration. When students or parents complain that homework is busy work, it may be that they don't see how the task connects to the learning, but often it is simply a task that doesn't work for them or that they don't need to do.

The antidote to this problem is to involve students in designing their own homework. If students know and understand the learning goals, they can choose from teacher-designed options or create homework assignments that work for their learning preferences. Teachers may also work with students to personalize tasks. Students can then assess the effectiveness of their tasks through self-assessment, teacher feedback, or no-count quizzes. Students as young as 1st graders have chosen their own homework tasks and learned how to assess the effectiveness of their methods (Vatterott, 2017).

Homework time and timing. Some of the most stressful aspects of homework are related to time. Many teachers and parents hold the misconception that the amount of homework is an indication of rigor. Heavy workload = rigor is a false equivalency and is not supported by the research (Vatterott, 2018). This belief, more than any other, is responsible for the piling on of hours of homework in many schools, and it is especially entrenched in high-achieving high schools in wealthy communities. Time spent on homework is not the metric for rigor; rigor is about complexity and the level of learning required. Excessive homework is a mental health issue, a sleep deprivation issue, and an equity issue. After all, students who have jobs, chores, or family members to care for can't spend hours on homework every night.

When we assign the same homework task to all students, we have another time problem. We know students differ in working speed: The same task that takes one student 20 minutes could take another student an hour or longer. Instead of expecting students who work more slowly to spend *more* time on a task, one solution is to put a reasonable time limit on each task—for example, "Don't spend more than 25 minutes on this set of problems." This practice not only reduces student and parent stress but also provides valuable feedback to the teacher about individual students' working speed and level of understanding.

Next, we have the 24-hour problem. Homework assigned on a Monday and due on Tuesday disregards student and family schedules and adds to student and parent stress. A better alternative is to give homework further in advance or to extend the amount of time students have to complete the work. This gives students and families much-needed flexibility to schedule homework around other outside activities. Some teachers use weekly packets, whereas others organize homework by the unit or provide a syllabus with all assignments and due dates for the semester.

Finally, we have a deadline problem. When missing a deadline is penalized with a lower grade, some students will stay up all night to complete the work, while others will simply take the poor grade. Both options are extremely stressful. There are many reasons why a student might miss a deadline, and they cannot all be written off as irresponsibility, lack of planning, or poor time management. If we are concerned about student stress, it makes sense for us to be flexible about deadlines. During the pandemic, "Grace before grades" became a common expression for allowing flexibility in assignment deadlines. There was a realization that given the stresses of the pandemic, perhaps teachers should extend some grace to students. Shouldn't we always have been doing that? Given the prevalence of student stress, it seems appropriate to continue to extend grace.

If we have already resolved the 24-hour problem, the frequency of the deadline problem will decrease. And, of course, moving to ungraded homework and reducing the amount of homework we assign would also make deadlines less of a problem.

For long-range projects, it is helpful to have intermittent deadlines for milestones along the progression of the task. This mitigates the tendency of students to procrastinate or to idealize how quickly the project will come together. When needed, the teacher could work with students to find a mutually agreeable due date, what one teacher called a "soft deadline."

The deadline problem is often exacerbated by a lack of coordination among teachers, which results in deadline overload. In a traditional high school schedule, students take courses from six to eight teachers, each of whom may assign homework and schedule exams and projects without consulting one another. To avoid overload, a shared calendar can help teachers track due dates for major projects and exams and make adjustments to give students some breathing room. (For more on effective homework practices, see *Rethinking Homework: Best Practices That Support Diverse Needs, 2nd Edition* [Vatterott, 2018].)

Challenges

Nobody said moving toward student autonomy in learning would be easy or perfect. For teachers, it involves a leap of faith to trust that students *can* take responsibility for learning when they have a voice in the process. The process does involve making mistakes and modeling failing forward to our students. Change is humbling, and the process can be messy. For both teachers and students, it requires unlearning old roles and learning new roles.

One of the biggest challenges is that many students don't know how to take charge of their learning—both because they've never been allowed to and because they've never had to. That lack of experience results in a lack of confidence in their ability to self-direct. School may have been boring before, but at least it was predictable: Students just had to do what they were told. Some high-achieving students might be so good at the traditional method that they end up being the ones most intimidated by having autonomy in their learning.

Because these skills are not innate, students do need to be taught how to take charge of their learning. The prerequisites are the relationships and practices discussed in this chapter, including the following:

- A nurturing learning environment where it's safe to make mistakes, ask for clarification, and request feedback
- A trusting teacher-student relationship
- Plenty of nonpunitive feedback from teachers and the freedom to ask other students for feedback
- Multiple opportunities to demonstrate mastery and time to fail forward

There are two other skills that students need to direct their own learning: an understanding of how they learn best and how to self-assess.

Students Need to Understand How They Learn

Students don't always think through how they learn best or what kind of explanation works well for them. If they do know, they may be reluctant to ask for the explanations they need out of fear that it makes them look stupid or weird. A simple survey such as the following would enable them to reflect on their preferred methods and dignify the different ways students learn:

Which of these sounds like the best way for you to understand something?

___ I need to see the big picture first.
___ I need a step-by-step plan of where to start.
___ I need to see the wrong way to do something, then see the right way.
___ I need to see examples and nonexamples.
___ I like to know the most common mistakes people make and the most common misconceptions people have.

Students Need to Learn How to Assess Their Own Learning

If students are to feel secure about directing their own learning, self-assessment is an essential skill. Because many students have little experience in this area, they benefit from some low-risk practice. A good way for them to start is to assess examples of someone else's learning.

In a 7th grade English language arts class, students work in groups and, using a rubric with scores 1 through 4, assess student papers from a previous semester. Then they defend their ratings. This exercise familiarizes them with the learning targets for the assignment and prepares them to use the rubric later to assess their own writing (Vatterott, 2018).

Many teachers use a dual rubric, where students self-assess their work and then the teacher assesses it. After some practice, students get better at the self-assessment process and more closely match the teachers' assessment.

Just as teachers new to student autonomy are more comfortable gradually incorporating autonomous activities into their classrooms, students need to take baby steps, too. For some students, especially those who excel at compliance and simply following instructions, too much autonomy too quickly can be overwhelming. At the Innovation Academy at Basehor-Linwood High School, teachers quickly realized that the freshman class needed step-by-step instructions, project examples, and one-on-one guidance to make decisions about their learning. They designed the freshman course to be teacher-centered with choices (revisit Figures 4.1 and 4.2 for a refresher on the continuums of student autonomy in learning). At each progressive grade level, the classes moved more to the right of the continuum, until by senior year, student projects were student-directed.

The teachers in the Innovation Academy course observed that some students never were quite comfortable making decisions about their learning, simply wanted to be told what to do, and needed a lot of hand-holding. Other students relished the autonomy and reenrolled each year in the course to experience new challenges.

Conclusion

Although we can't control the outside elements that cause stress in our students, there is much we can do in the classroom to lighten students' school-related stress load. We can begin by building relationships and targeting the stress that comes from traditional norms and learning, grading, and homework practices and mitigate it by allowing autonomy and flexibility. When we revamp those practices to give students more control, we not only reduce stress but also increase engagement and help students to become successful, self-directed learners. And isn't that our goal?

School should be a refuge from the stressors of the other worlds teens live in, a place where they can define themselves and feel comfortable. Providing and sustaining the mental health support that students need requires adults and students alike to embrace new roles. Chapter 5 illustrates how schools can create an environment that cultivates this support.

5

Schoolwide Wellness Practices, Policies, and Programs

So far, we've explored the unique developmental needs of adolescents, the shift in practice needed to create less stressful schools and classrooms and support student well-being, and how to create the optimal classroom environment. But deep, lasting change happens at the building and district levels.

With the relentless pressure on schools to achieve high standardized test scores and the hyperfocus on achievement, it's been easy to take our eye off what matters most: helping children grow into healthy, well-adjusted adults. The wellness paradigm outlined in Chapter 3 is our ultimate goal, and adolescents' developmental and human needs are the lighthouse guiding the schoolwide practices, policies, and programs that will get us to that goal.

Our Commitment to the Whole Child

As educators, our job is not just academics, and it never has been. We have always been focused on the whole child: concerned about our students' physical and emotional health as well as their achievement. We care physically for kids when they are sick, we feed those who are hungry, and we find coats and shoes for those who need them. We comfort students when they are in distress, and we are mandated reporters for abuse or neglect. From there, it's a short leap to caring about their mental health and well-being. Especially now, we understand that mental health is a prerequisite for academic achievement.

Think about what is involved when we make a commitment to our own physical health. We commit to making changes, like exercising, that become part of our routine. We make decisions based on that commitment, like choosing healthier foods. We monitor our health by checking our blood pressure and keeping doctor appointments and, if we are serious, we commit to a long-range plan.

When we commit to student well-being, we make similar changes. We shift our focus from primarily academic support to both academic and mental health support. We prioritize students' developmental needs and relationships and make decisions based on those priorities. We change our practices and routines to support student wellness. And—the focus of this chapter—we make a commitment at an organizational level, creating structures and practices that normalize mental health support, with the expectation that wellness is everyone's job. It takes a village and a commitment of the village to a long-range plan. Many of the practices shared in this chapter were developed by schools over several years of sustained commitment to student wellness.

Four components must work together symbiotically at the building level for student wellness to flourish:

- *Power:* Empowering students to be full partners in decisions that affect their school
- *Time:* Giving students time during the school day and beyond to meet their needs for connection, competence, and time to explore and discover their unique identity

- *Support:* Providing mental health support that is respectful, accessible, and accepted as a normal school service
- *Knowledge:* Educating teachers, students, and parents about the basics of mental health, well-being, and self-care

Wellness Needs Power

Chapter 4 demonstrated how student autonomy in the learning process can meet students' developmental needs, reduce stress, and improve engagement. Students benefit in the same ways when they are given a voice in other aspects of their school experience. They are entitled to weigh in on decisions that affect their lives.

If we are committed to student wellness, we must be willing to listen to our students. When we provide opportunities for students to be heard, we find out what they need and what is important to them, we address their developmental needs of belonging and connection, and we send the message that students are central to the school organization.

Traditionally, student voice has been limited to controlled formats like surveys or focus groups, in which students function as a source of data or as respondents; they are not involved in decision making (Eccles, 2024). Only when student voice is acted on by the school do students come to believe that their voice actually counts.

At Thomas Kelly College Preparatory School in Chicago, student surveys revealed that most students didn't believe the teachers cared about them and didn't think the content they were learning was relevant. This feedback led to the next school year's initiative, "Meaningful Work," which caused teachers to make changes in instruction (Stone, 2024b). The school also created Freshman Café, an end-of-year event for freshmen in which students met one-on-one with an adult for 5 to 10 minutes to give feedback on how the year had gone and to ask questions about sophomore year (Stone, 2024c).

When we increase the level of student involvement in the workings of the school, such as by forming student committees, we send the message that students' role in the school is not to be cogs in a wheel, but to be contributing members of the organization. This increased power and responsibility for students meets other developmental needs related to identity, helping students answer the questions *Who am I? What am I good at? What do I care about? How can I make a difference?*

At Hardin Middle School in St. Charles, Missouri, students are elected by their advisory class or appointed by their teacher to serve on the Principals Advisory Committee. At their monthly meetings with Dr. Jewett, the principal, they bring concerns from their advisory class on such topics as students pushing others on the steps or a lack of options for lunch. "No issue is dismissed; they are all acted on," the principal said. When the students complained that the water in the drinking fountain tasted funny, Dr. Jewett had the water tested. When the committee reported that some urinal dividers were missing in the boys' restroom (an important concern for middle school boys), Dr. Jewett worked with the custodian to resolve the problem within a few days.

The students on the committee also communicate information from the principal to their student groups. Each month, Dr. Jewett creates a slideshow in simple language about a topic she wants students to know about, such as why the state test is important, or what the latest attendance initiative is. She introduces the slideshow to the committee and takes questions. The following week, the students present the slideshow to their classmates.

"People keep saying, 'Why don't you just let your assistant principal meet with the committee?' But the students need me—they need to know that they are that important," Dr. Jewett said. In this school, student voice has become real power.

The ultimate demonstration of student power is when students lead an initiative or partner with adults to solve problems in their school (Eccles, 2024). In the Phoenix Union High School District in Phoenix, Arizona, students control a portion of the school's budget through participatory budgeting, similar to the practice used by municipal governments whereby community members vote on how to spend public funds. Students submit ideas for how to spend a sum of money, and all students vote to determine which ideas are funded. In the past, students have voted to fund more comfortable seats, device-charging stations, and a canopy to shade outdoor seating (Lieberman, 2023).

At Village School in Colorado Springs, Colorado, students organize all clubs and all social events, including Homecoming, Fall Festival, and Prom. The students wanted a volleyball team and, with the principal's blessing, took control of all the administrative details and permissions to make it happen. "We believe the school belongs to the students, so they have a loud voice in what we do," said the principal.

At William Mason High School in Mason, Ohio, student voice is a prominent force in creating a supportive and inclusive environment at the school. With an ethnically diverse student population and more than 75 languages spoken in the community, the student leadership team has organized community book studies for books such as *Subtle Acts of Exclusion: How to Understand, Identify, and Stop Microaggressions* (Jana & Baran, 2020); sponsored various cultural heritage activities; conducted anti-bias training for students; and led professional development for teachers. They have created teacher resources including student surveys and a bank of ideas for how to connect with students. They also interview teacher candidates and provide feedback to the administration.

When students have this level of power within their school and work with others toward a common goal, they build relationships with peers and adults, again enhancing their sense of belonging. As they take responsibility, they meet their need for competence and gain the satisfaction of doing meaningful work.

Wellness Needs Time

When we are committed to student wellness, we reorganize the school schedule to better meet students' developmental needs. Adolescents need time during the school day to connect with others, consistently and frequently. But they also need downtime to process, reflect on, and grapple with problems. A typical student schedule is hardly conducive to meeting any of these needs. Students often juggle six to eight classes each day, and then, to add to the craziness, they often have no more than five minutes to travel between classes and shift their focus from one subject to the next. Is that for the benefit of the teachers or the students, or is it simply unquestioned tradition? Who would want to navigate this schedule every day?

Adding Minutes to Passing Time and the Lunch Period

We can begin by slowing the manic pace of the day. Two of the easiest ways to remove stress from the schedule are to add minutes to passing time and lunchtime. Extending passing time between classes from the typical 3 minutes to 8–10 minutes helps students feel less rushed and gives them time to say hello to friends and use the restroom (Miles et al., 2022; Vatterott, 2024). Expanding this time by just a few minutes gives students enough space to breathe and shift gears to be ready for their next class. Administrators I've spoken to report that those extra minutes have been a game changer in terms of student stress level.

Not all schools actually require a designated lunch period for students: In some schools, students are allowed to pack their schedules so full that they don't have a lunch period at all. For student well-being, however, it's important to designate and protect a mandatory lunch period. That period should be long enough to enable students to eat and interact with others, meeting both nutritional and social needs. The CDC recommends that students have at least 20 minutes of "seat time" to sit and eat, which in most schools would require a lunch period of 30 minutes or more. In a nationally represented survey, 9 out of 10 teachers agreed that their students need at least a half-hour to eat (Sparks & Prothero, 2023). Researchers found that the longer lunch period resulted in students eating more fruits and vegetables, leading to healthier eating habits (Burg et al., 2021).

Providing Blocks of Academic Time

Traditional secondary schedules often lack sufficient time to accommodate student differences in learning, resulting in some students who struggle to learn or just need more time to learn. The purpose of providing blocks of academic time is to promote mastery and enable learners to experience competence in academics as well as to provide enrichment for students who master the content easily and quickly. A popular concept in middle schools is WIN (What I Need) time. Mattoon Middle School in Mattoon, Illinois, allots 40 minutes daily for WIN time, which is used for remediation, enrichment, or student goal setting.

Another scheduling option is academic lab, usually one period a day (or every other day in a block schedule). Students are assigned to a specific teacher for academic lab but typically have the freedom to visit other teachers for help or to make up work, similar to teacher office hours. Students may also use that time as study hall to work on homework or long-range assignments. In some high schools, teachers keep the same academic lab students for all four years, promoting closer teacher-student relationships. Administrators may prioritize the scheduling of some students, such as English language learners or students with individualized education plans, to allow them to be placed with the teacher most likely to be able to help them. For example, a special education student who struggles with math may be assigned to a math teacher for academic lab, so that they don't need to leave to visit their math teacher. English language learners may be assigned to their ELL teacher or a foreign language teacher who speaks their native language.

Providing Blocks of Nonacademic Time

Many schools include nonacademic blocks of time such as advisory periods to facilitate both teacher-student relationships and peer relationships. An advisory period can be an important resource for social-emotional learning, class meetings, and one-on-one check-ins. The advisory teacher typically has access to academic and attendance data and can review grades and attendance with individual students. As one student said, "We do better when we have people doing those one-on-one check-ins" (Stone, 2024a, p. 5). "[Students] want the teacher to talk to them, and they want them to tell them how they're doing," said one administrator (Stone, 2024b, p. 9).

At South View Middle School in Edina, Minnesota, advisory groups are multi-age, and teachers keep the same students for all three years, which offers several advantages. First, the teachers develop long-term relationships with students—not only do they have the satisfaction of watching the students mature, but they also get a longitudinal picture of who the student is. "If you only see the student as an 8th grader, when they can get a little stubborn, you may think that's who they are. But if you've have known the student for two years and watched them mature, you realize this is just a particular stage they are going through," said the principal. Being in a class of 6th, 7th, and 8th graders is ideal for middle school students to form peer relationships. At a time when students' physical, social, and emotional development can span a five-year period from early bloomers to late bloomers, a slow-maturing 8th grader may connect well with a faster-maturing 6th grader. Seventh and 8th grade students can also serve as mentors to 6th graders, sometimes leading advisory and helping them with new challenges such as lockers and schedules.

Some schools offer a single block of time that serves both academic and nonacademic purposes. At Hardin Middle School, academic lab period is used for academic intervention, enrichment, class meetings, and teacher check-ins with students.

Providing Flex Time

Flex time, as the name implies, is flexible in its use, based on student need or choice. In many schools, flex time is more like academic lab, and student choices are limited to academics. At South View Middle School, flex time is a 35-minute period offered every day and offers many more options for students. All teachers have a flex period, many offering support or enrichment. Subject-area teachers sometimes work together to differentiate their flex periods. For instance, one math teacher may offer retesting or support, while another provides enrichment activities. Although normally students choose their flex, teachers can also schedule a student into their flex, which overrides the student's choice. As one teacher said, "You can pull in the kids you really need to see." Here are some examples of the wide variety of daily flex sessions offered at South View Middle School:

- Spanish 7—study for test
- Physical Earth project work
- Writer's workshop
- 7th grade language arts support
- Monday motivation workout
- Yearbook work session
- 7th grade full band

In the true spirit of flexibility, flex time at South View is scheduled each day immediately following the 20-minute advisory period. This allows the two periods (plus the 3 minutes between classes) to be combined occasionally for a 58-minute block of time for clubs or other special events. Once a month, advisory and flex are combined for belonging clubs. Every spring and fall, students complete interest surveys and adults offer suggestions for these multi-age clubs. Led by teachers or other adults, the club themes are as varied as LEGO, Calling All Swifties, Fly Fishing, Gardening, Disney Fans, and Yoga. Teachers or staff members choose to create or lead clubs based on their interests, and the students are sometimes surprised that their teachers are excited about the same hobbies that they are. "It's so rewarding for me to see the kids outside the classroom," one teacher said. The students also enjoy making new friends who have similar interests.

Providing Autonomous Time

Autonomous time is time during the school day that students may choose to spend how they wish. Blocks of time such as advisory, academic lab, or study hall are important because they give students a break from formal instruction, but how that time is used and structured determines whether it is truly autonomous time. If advisory period is used to offer planned, required social-emotional learning, then that is not autonomous time. If the study hall rules dictate that students must remain seated, quiet, and focused on their work, then that is not autonomous time, either. Existing blocks such as advisory or academic lab can, however, be repurposed to be autonomous time, if they are flexible enough to allow students choices. If it is truly autonomous time, students are free to work on homework or other assignments, travel to meet with teachers, visit with school counselors, or do nothing at all. A 20–60-minute block of time is ideal (Miles et al., 2022) because it is long enough to be restorative and affords students greater access to teachers and other support staff.

Autonomous time may be part of an extended lunch hour or scheduled contiguous to a lunch period. Organizing this extra time could be as simple as offering students two or three choices at the end of the lunch period—for example, a quiet classroom, the gym, or the library. At

Mattoon Middle School, students have a 40-minute block of time—20 minutes for lunch and 20 minutes for recess, during which they may play outside or in the gym. James E. Dottke High School in West Allis, Wisconsin, has implemented what it calls Flex 40 lunch:

> During "Flex 40," a 40-minute lunch period, students can pick almost any space in the school to relax and recharge. They might play music, shoot baskets on the basketball court, or just sit in a classroom. (Vatterott, 2022, para. 20)

At William Mason High School, students have a unique block of autonomous time every Wednesday. During the weekly 70-minute Connect Time, students sign up for teacher-facilitated activities ranging from jewelry making to karaoke. The teachers believe Connect Time offers an important break for students while strengthening teacher-student relationships. "Our students work really hard and are in a lot of activities," one administrator said. "Connect Time is like recess for high school students." Interestingly, the principal noted that quiet time is the option most requested by students.

Rethinking Student Schedule Choices

We have all had times when we had too much on our plates and complained, "There aren't enough hours in the day!" To emphasize the importance of work-life balance, it is helpful to require students to take a realistic look at their schedule and do the math to see if it's balanced and sustainable. Challenge Success (2021), a Stanford-based organization that works with schools, created a time management worksheet (available at https://challengesuccess.org/resources/time-management) that has students list time requirements for academics, extracurriculars, and daily living activities such as eating and sleeping. (It features a prominent message that the American Academy of Pediatrics recommends 8–10 hours of sleep nightly, and the form is prepopulated with 9 hours of sleep a night.) Prior to the students completing the worksheet, teachers submit estimated workloads for all courses.

The time management form is a powerful tool to reveal to students which activities may not fit into a 168-hour week, and to think through their schedule: *Are those four AP classes really manageable? How much homework can I expect? How many days a week will the team or the orchestra practice? What would it feel like to get 8–10 hours of sleep?* After completing the form, students share it with their parents and possibly rethink some of their decisions for the next semester.

Other Possible Scheduling Changes

Most educators are familiar with early dismissal days and late-start days designed to give students the gift of time. Schools are experimenting with other options designed to make the student schedule less stressful. Some schools are offering one day a week of distance learning as mental health relief. The day is designed not for virtual instruction but for independent study and catching up on what students decide they need to work on, but it also allows students to sleep in. Another scheduling option is the 4x4 semester, in which students take four courses in four extended blocks each day. Taking fewer courses at a time enables students to complete four courses each semester, similar to a college schedule. Finally, a school may limit advanced placement classes by offering a limited number, not offering them at all, or setting a cap on how many AP classes a student may take in a semester or year.

Some educators may see changing the school schedule as just plain undoable. After all, schedules for elementary, middle, and high schools fit together like puzzle pieces, and often the bus schedule drives it all. School schedules are complex, and it's sometimes hard to think outside the box. But creative thinkers with solid rationales for change have managed to do so, many by repurposing existing structures like study hall or advisory, changing course offerings, or adopting a block or modified block schedule. Visit unlockingtime.org for a wealth of innovative scheduling ideas.

Wellness Needs Support

The traditional paradigm for addressing student mental health is reactive: A mental health concern is viewed as a problem to be fixed, and typically only students with serious problems are helped. As we move toward a wellness paradigm, we can look beyond "fixing" behaviors and alleviating symptoms to addressing some of the root causes. The wellness paradigm addresses mental health challenges proactively and views mental health as part of overall health. *All* students are served, and wellness is not the sole province of mental health professionals—all adults in the school have a role to play. Adolescents need caring adults to show them that just as everyone gets sick sometimes, everyone experiences mental health challenges from time to time. In the wellness paradigm, mental health support is normalized and destigmatized. Support strategies may consist of policies to address stress-inducing school practices and tools to detect students who are struggling as well as those who may be experiencing a more serious mental health crisis.

Policy as Support

When we look proactively at student mental health, we may discover that some of our academic practices are unwittingly contributing to student stress. Although Chapter 4 outlined how individual teachers can change classroom practices to reduce student stress, it is much more powerful, and speaks to administrative commitment, when schools create buildingwide policies or guidelines. High school students list grades, tests and other assessments, homework, and overall workload as their top sources of school stress (Challenge Success & NBC News, 2021). Although teachers can implement many strategies to reduce stress for students in these areas (again, see Chapter 4), the problem for students is often the lack of consistency from their multiple teachers. It is not uncommon, especially in high school, for teachers to have considerable latitude in how they grade and what they choose to include in the grade. For instance, individual teachers may weight exams and homework differently and may award or deduct points for student behaviors such as attendance or absence, punctuality or tardiness, or turning work in on time or late. These discrepancies can lead to a dizzying array of grading schemes that students must consider when they encounter multiple deadlines from their various teachers. Which teacher enacts the harshest penalty for a late project? Which teachers allow retakes or revisions? How much does homework count in this class versus that class?

Some grading stress can be relieved with schoolwide policies that improve grading consistency among teachers. One such set of practices is known as *standards-based grading,* also called *grading for learning* or *equitable grading practices* (Feldman, 2019; Vatterott, 2015). Standards-based grading is a mastery-based system of reporting learning progress that removes nonacademic factors from the grade. But it is not necessary for a school to convert to standards-based grading to adopt some commonsense practices that give students more control over their grades and more time to demonstrate mastery. Schoolwide policies or guidelines provide more consistency for students and reinforce the wellness paradigm's commitment to reducing student stress. Here are some examples of different grading policies that schools have adopted:

- Students have multiple opportunities to demonstrate learning through formative assessment, assessment retakes, or revisions of work. Recent evidence of learning will replace old evidence, not be averaged with it.
- Absences and tardiness will be tracked and reported but not included in the grade.
- "Academic dishonesty (cheating) will be addressed as a *disciplinary* concern. Students who are found to have engaged in academic dishonesty will be required to provide evidence of their actual level of learning" (Vatterott, 2015, p. 108).

Limiting the degree to which homework counts in the grade is also an important policy to reduce student stress because individual teachers vary widely in how much weight they assign to homework in the grade. One high school principal surveyed his teachers and found the percentage homework counted in the quarter grade ranged from 10 percent to 90 percent! The more homework counts in the grade, teachers observe, the more stressed students become and the more likely they are to cheat. Here are examples of different homework policies that schools have adopted:

- "Formative practice homework does not count in the grade, but summative assignments (such as research papers) may count within the [maximum 20 percent] limit" (Vatterott, 2018, p. 182).

- "Homework may count a maximum of 10 percent in the quarter grade" (Vatterott, 2018, p. 182).
- Homework may count from 0 percent to 20 percent of the quarter grade.
- "Homework may not be counted in the grade but will be reported in the Work Habits section of the report card" (Vatterott, 2018, p. 182).

Schools that have implemented standards-based grading often adopt the last policy in the list and no longer count homework in the grade (Vatterott, 2019). When schools limit homework's impact on the grade, students are able to make decisions about which homework tasks are most helpful for their learning and that they may choose to complete.

Other aspects of homework that cause stress—the amount of time homework requires and the uniformity of the tasks assigned—were detailed in Chapter 4, but it bears repeating that a heavy workload is not an indication of rigor. Excessive homework compromises students' physical and mental health and interferes with a balanced life of family time, downtime, leisure time, and sleep. Most troubling is the relationship between excessive homework and sleep deprivation. When homework robs students of adequate sleep, it exacerbates anxiety and depression. It is critical to student well-being that homework issues be addressed.

Some schools offer a homework-free weekend once a month, which is welcome but does little to alleviate persistent homework stress and load. Ideally, every weekend should be a homework-free weekend. Under that policy, homework would be assigned Monday through Thursday only, no homework would be due on Monday, and no tests would be given on Monday. Many schools are now mandating homework-free school holidays and homework-free school breaks. Another popular practice has been to push back the fall semester so that final exams occur before Christmas, allowing students to have a work-free break (Vatterott, 2019). Other policies include limiting the amount of homework that can be assigned in each class, limiting the amount of time students are expected to spend on homework each night, and giving students more than one day to complete assignments. Some schools prohibit disciplinary punishments such as isolated lunch or detention for incomplete homework.

Coordination of Workload Across Classes

To help students manage their time and to protect them from overload, it makes sense that teachers would coordinate student workload. This is usually easier at the middle school level because students have fewer options for academic courses. If a middle school organizes students and teachers into interdisciplinary teams, the four core subject-area teachers share the same 100–150 students and typically have common planning periods, making it relatively easy to coordinate tests and major projects. High school coordination gets trickier, with a potentially infinite number of student schedules and teachers who may not share common planning time. For high schools and middle schools not organized in teams, teachers may be required to post due dates for major projects, exams, and events on a common calendar. If needed, the administration can limit the number of exams or major projects per day or week. Another option, common at colleges and universities, is allowing students to reschedule an exam if they have more than two exams scheduled on the same day. Does the common calendar impinge on teacher freedom? Sometimes, yes. But the school's priority must always be students' well-being.

A complete shared calendar should also include time commitments for extracurricular events. Although most teachers would be aware of these, it is helpful to include intensive pre-performance schedules for concerts, school plays, or big games.

Programs for Stress Reduction and Self-Regulation

Some of the more common mental health supports are more reactive than proactive, but they are helpful nonetheless and better than nothing. Many schools now offer programs focused on mindfulness, meditation, or breathing exercises to help students cope with stress. Although such programs are beneficial, they are treating the symptoms rather than addressing the causes of stress.

Other common supports are in-the-moment interventions and self-regulation spaces, designed to help students who are overwhelmed emotionally. Traditionally, problem behavior was viewed as a discipline issue and handled by dealing out some kind of consequence. A more respectful approach is to view problem behavior as a sign of a student's temporary need to regain their equilibrium—of self-regulation that needs to be developed. In the Cherry Creek School District in the metropolitan Denver area, schools using self-regulation spaces in response to behavioral problems in lieu of office referrals saw a significant drop in referrals.

Many schools now have these spaces, sometimes called Zen dens, where students can take a break from the day or get mental health assistance before returning to class. Here, students can be taught to pay attention to signals their body gives them and steps to take, such as deep breathing, to help them self-regulate. Interestingly, one principal said that most students don't even need to talk to an adult, just 20 minutes of quiet alone time (Superville, 2023a).

A Zen den is often attached to the guidance counselor's office or a student wellness center and staffed by a wellness coordinator. At Westlake High School in Saratoga Springs, Utah, the Zen den is housed in a larger wellness center and features such amenities as adult coloring books, a miniature Zen garden, and a weighted blanket (the students' favorite) to help students relax and decompress. The wellness center functions as "a triage for the counseling center at the school," as one principal put it (Superville, 2023a, para. 28), to determine whether a student needs to talk with someone or just needs solitude. Wellness coordinators could be social workers, licensed family counselors, or other mental health professionals (Superville, 2023a). Students may come to a wellness center for any number of reasons—problems with a friend, parents who are fighting or divorcing, or just a stressful day when everything goes wrong.

Self-regulation does not always require a designated space; many teachers have learned that the solution to a problem behavior or outburst may be as simple as allowing the student a short break ("Go get a drink and walk up and down the hall for a minute"). The goal is for students to regain their composure. Don't we all "need a moment" sometimes?

If self-regulation is a persistent problem for a particular student, then the issue merits investigating: Why are they so easily knocked off balance, what is preventing them from self-regulating, and what coping strategies might help? That investigative work requires moving to the next level of support by engaging in practices that require a little more work to implement. Those practices are tailored to individual students and could include self-regulation training, physical health evaluation, testing for learning disabilities, or screening for depression or substance abuse.

Relationships as Support

Although practices for stress reduction and self-regulation are helpful, they can't come close to the value of personal relationships. Our goal should be to surround students with caring adults and peers and to create conditions that allow relationships to flourish. Many schools have implemented a Choose a Trusted Adult program at the start of each year. Typically, after students have had a few weeks to get to know the adults in the school, they are given a sheet picturing all the adults in the building and asked to choose an adult whom they would feel comfortable going to with a problem. (A brief "about me" summary for each adult would also be helpful.) Some schools have partnered with One Trusted Adult (one trustedadult.com), a research-based program that offers an advisory curriculum and training for adults and students.

At Colleyville Middle School in Colleyville, Texas, the teachers and staff have access to a "data wall," a form of relationship mapping that lists each student and, next to each name, the initials of the trusted adult whom the student has chosen. If a student does not select an adult, it's a sign that an adult needs to make a connection (Stone, 2024a). At Mattoon Middle School, students are asked to identify two trusted adults, including one at their grade level. Village School has an unusual method of matching students with a caring adult: At the beginning of the school year, teachers create a commercial about themselves, sharing their interests and what type of mentor they will be. Students then select a teacher to be their mentor. The number of students is capped at 30 for each teacher, but students may "break up" with a mentor and select a different one if they feel their mentor is not a good fit.

Many schools, especially middle schools, have implemented advisory periods, and it is becoming more common for teachers to keep the same advisees for multiple years. South View Middle School has a unique structure for developing trusted student-adult relationships. As previously discussed, a 20-minute advisory period is built into the daily schedule adjacent to the 35-minute flex time, which may be used to extend advisory time or for academic purposes. Advisory groups are multi-age (6th–8th grade) and small (only about 18 students), and teachers keep the same advisees for three years. Wednesdays and Thursdays are reserved for one-on-one check-ins. On those days, while the teacher checks in with individual students, the other students have Connect Time, device-free time during which they play board games donated by community members. The advisory teacher has access to all their advisees' records, including grades, attendance, and any behavioral referrals. This not only enables teachers to get to know their students better and build stronger relationships but also gives parents one teacher to contact who has a complete picture of how the student is doing.

Peer relationships are just as important as adult relationships in supporting student mental health. Organized and trained groups of students can help to create a positive, caring school climate. Sources of Strength (sourcesofstrength.org), a student leadership program many school districts have adopted, trains peer leaders (working with adult advisors) to engage in positive messaging about hope, resilience, strength, and trusted adults. Their messaging campaigns encourage help-seeking behaviors and healthy coping. SPEAK (Students Promoting Emotional Awareness & Kindness) is a student mental health leadership advisory committee in Littleton Public Schools (LPS) in Littleton, Colorado. The committee focuses on student wellness and engagement, suicide prevention, and social-emotional support. When the district began creating a digital mental health curriculum for middle and high school students, the committee helped pick topics and gave feedback to the graphic designers.

Hope Squad (hopesquad.com) is a peer counseling program used in thousands of schools in the United States and Canada. The Hope Squad at Hilliard Davidson High School in Ohio partners student volunteers with adults to serve as a mental health resource for other students. Students serve on Hope Squad not as formal counselors, but to act as watchdogs and compassionate listeners. Hope Squad students are trained to spot peers with mental health struggles and persuade them to get help from a trusted adult or, in some cases, refer them to adult support. As one Hope Squad member said, "From our training, we learn the red flags to watch for. Once we know what [students] need, we're just guiding them towards it" (Gewertz, 2022, para. 4). At William Mason High School, also in Ohio, Hope Squad is offered as a course for elective credit. Administrators credit the Hope Squad program with encouraging more students to seek help and raising teacher awareness of student mental health issues.

Attendance Monitoring

One of the most proactive steps educators can take to support student mental health is to closely monitor attendance. Excessive absenteeism can be a red flag for mental health challenges, and conversely, consistent attendance can serve as a protective factor for student well-being. Regular school attendance not only meets student developmental needs for belonging and adult and peer relationships but is also critical for academic success.

Absenteeism should not be approached as an attendance issue but investigated by a caring adult. The student should be supported by interventions, not subjected to traditional punitive measures. Ideally, trusted adults should take charge of connecting with the student and their parents to learn what is contributing to the absences. As one administrator said, "We believe the relationship is the intervention" (Stone, 2024b, p. 10).

The first step in investigating absenteeism is to rule out factors related to the student's living situation, such as transportation challenges, lack of clean clothes, or obligations to care for younger siblings or work to provide for their family. Those issues require different supports than academic, social, or emotional causes of absenteeism and would typically involve social services working with the family.

Many factors that contribute to absenteeism are related to bullying, the student's sense of belonging, other peer problems, or academic frustration. If a student is not doing well in school either academically or socially, they may not go to school simply to avoid a painful situation. Unfortunately, a vicious circle can develop: The more the student avoids school, the bigger the gaps in instruction get, making it harder to learn. And the more a student is absent, the less likely other students are to develop and strengthen friendships with them. What group of students will continue to welcome a student who seldom shows up? Both learning and relationships are damaged by chronic absenteeism, leading to greater academic frustration, increased social isolation, and a gradual disengagement from school. Now the absenteeism itself has contributed to poor student mental health. When the cause of absenteeism is anxiety-related, avoidance reinforces the anxiety, and another vicious circle emerges.

Effective attendance monitoring requires early intervention, such as a system for an automatic intervention after a given number of absences. At Mattoon Middle School, an intervention is triggered at five absences and again at seven absences. Both interventions are handled by one of the student's trusted adults. When the student has missed five days, the adult meets with the student and reaches out to the parent to discover the cause or causes of the absences. When the student has missed seven days, the communication becomes, "We need a plan." The adult and student work together to form such a plan (one student just needed a second alarm clock) and communicate it to the parents.

Student Mental Health Days

At least a dozen U.S. states now permit student mental health days as excused absences, and the number of school districts allowing mental health days is growing (Prothero, 2023). By allowing student mental health days, schools show students that mental health is as important as physical health. Policies differ from school to school and from state to state about such details as whether a doctor's note is required, how many mental health days are allowed (two to five days a school year is common), and what school interventions may be triggered after a certain number of mental health days are taken. Some schools use a special absence code to indicate a mental health day, so counselors or social workers can track the absences and reach out to students and families.

A student may need a mental health day simply to rest and recharge, or to process a stressful event like a break-up or the loss of a pet. It is important to educate both students and parents about how and when a mental health day is needed, how to best use the day to support mental health, and the fact that a mental health day is no substitute for mental health support (Jacobson et al., 2025). It's also important for students and parents to realize that when we do not attend to our mental health, our immune systems weaken, making it more likely that we will get sick—which could result in a longer absence than if we had taken a day to de-stress.

Wellness Screening

Universal student wellness screenings are a proactive tool for managing student mental health and for early identification of potential mental health problems (Stanford, 2023). Psychological or social problems in adolescents often go unnoticed by teachers, pediatricians, and even parents. According to one administrator,

> Teachers are great at finding externalizing kids—the kids that are throwing something, disrupting class, fighting; that's easy for educators to see. . . . The kids that are being lost when you're not doing screening are the internalizing kids, the kids with anxiety, depression, school phobia, lack of social skills, or lack of friendships. (Stanford, 2023, p. 4)

Screeners help us identify adolescents with mental health problems so that we can address those problems before they become more serious, putting the students at risk for disciplinary issues or dropping out of school (Gall et al., 2000).

The American Academy of Pediatrics (along with other children's health organizations) recommends psychosocial screenings as a part of an annual physical (Massachusetts General Hospital Department of Psychiatry, n.d.). But because not all adolescents have access to a pediatrician, it seems appropriate and equitable that such screening be provided by schools.

Two of the most widely used school-based psychosocial screeners are the Behavior Intervention Monitoring Assessment System (BIMAS-2) (McDougal et al., 2020) and the Pediatric Symptom Checklist (PSC) (Jellinek et al., 1988). The BIMAS-2 (https://edumetrisis.com/bimas-2) asks students to rate the frequency of 34 behaviors, feelings, and interactions with others over the previous week. This gives educators a snapshot in time that can be compared with previous responses; this is typically conducted twice each school year (see Figure 5.1 for sample items).

Figure 5.1
Sample BIMAS-2 Questions

During the past week, I . . .	Never	Rarely	Some-times	Often	Very Often
1. Felt angry					
2. Did something risky					
3. Had trouble paying attention					
4. Was friendly with others					
5. Was sad or withdrawn					
6. Worked out problems with others					
7. Fought with others (verbally, physically, or both)					

Source: Sample items from J. L. McDougal, A. N. Bardos, & S. T. Meier, 2020, Behavior Intervention Monitoring Assessment System (BIMAS-2). Copyright 2020 Edumetrisis LLC.

The Pediatric Symptom Checklist—Youth Report (Y-PSC; www.massgeneral.org/assets/mgh/pdf/psychiatry/psc/psc-y-english.pdf) (Jellinek & Murphy, 1988) is used for adolescents. The Y-PSC covers physical health, mental health, and social and emotional well-being (see Figure 5.2 for sample items).

Both screeners quantify answers with points and suggest a numerical threshold for further action on the part of the school. Interventions may include training in self-regulation or social skills, evaluation for special education or 504 status, cognitive behavioral therapy, or referral to the school psychologist. For some students, further assessment may be warranted to screen for more serious mental disorders such as depression, suicidal ideation, or substance abuse.

> **Figure 5.2**
> **Sample Y-PSC Questions**
>
> Please mark under the heading that best fits you:
>
> | | Never | Sometimes | Often |
> |---|---|---|---|
> | Tire easily, little energy | ___ | ___ | ___ |
> | Have trouble sleeping | ___ | ___ | ___ |
> | Are irritable, angry | ___ | ___ | ___ |
> | Worry a lot | ___ | ___ | ___ |
> | Fight with other children | ___ | ___ | ___ |
> | Do not understand other people's feelings | ___ | ___ | ___ |
>
> *Source:* Sample items from M. Jellinek & J. M. Murphy, 1988, Pediatric Symptom Checklist (youth self-report version). Massachusetts General Hospital. Copyright 1988 M. Jellinek & J. M. Murphy.

The Cherry Creek School District administers an optional social-emotional learning (SEL) self-assessment to all students in grades 3–12. The assessment helps students to gauge their social-emotional skills, such as self-efficacy and social awareness, and to determine who might need more support building resiliency and identifying trusted adults. Although all students are exposed to an SEL curriculum, students who self-identify as low on five to seven competencies, such as sense of belonging and self-regulation, are flagged for additional help. The question, as one school mental health provider noted, is "Is something else going on?"

Signs of Suicide (SOS) is a tool used in many districts to inform both adults and students about suicide. After the student SOS program is conducted, students complete a form asking them to react to the information and share their own feelings or concerns about other students. In this way, the program serves as a screener for signs of depression or suicidal ideation.

Any type of universal screener must be administered with parental permission and within the limits of parental rights. Some parents may object to such screeners, and we cannot override parents' wishes, even if they conflict with our values. Note that parental permission may be either *opt-in* (i.e., parents must give permission for their child to be assessed) or *opt-out* (i.e., parents must request that their child not take the assessment). Most districts have a higher participation rate when using the opt-out option. (Cherry Creek uses an opt-out process for its SEL screening.) Even though the state of Ohio mandates that all students in grades 9–12 receive training in suicide prevention, parents have the right to opt out of that training if they believe it is inappropriate or traumatic for their child. In Olentangy Schools in Lewis Center, Ohio, student screening for depression is available, but parents must opt in if they wish their child to be screened.

For schools that wish to implement universal student mental health screening, the National Center for School Mental Health at the University of Maryland School of Medicine (2025) offers the School Health Assessment and Performance Evaluation (SHAPE) System, a free step-by-step action plan for implementing a student mental health screening process (https://www.schoolmentalhealth.org/shape/shape-assessments).

Crisis Support

For all our efforts to proactively address student wellness, there will always be students who experience crisis and require specialized support. To meet the needs of these students, many school districts have hired additional crisis counselors, social workers, or psychologists and redesigned their websites to provide extensive mental health resources. A robust website has resources organized in a user-friendly way with plain language (and often translated into multiple languages).

At the very least, school district websites should include links to suicide hotlines, anonymous tip lines to report concerns about students who may be a threat to themselves or others, and resources to connect students and parents to therapists. Some districts offer an online platform for "checking in" for immediate help and online counseling. This service functions as an urgent care center for student mental health. (For an example of a well-designed district website for student mental health, visit www.cherrycreekschools.org/mentalhealth.)

In an effort to serve students in need and lessen the disruption to their education, some districts provide a short-term therapeutic and transitional educational setting for students who would otherwise be out of school for mental health treatment. These programs are often conducted in partnership with local mental health providers or nonprofit agencies. Traverse Academy operates in the Cherry Creek School District as a first-of-its-kind mental health facility school for students. Upon admission to the program, students receive therapeutic care integrated with customized educational programming.

Partnerships and Foundations

In their commitment to the well-being of all students, more and more school districts are partnering with care providers in their communities in a variety of arrangements. Partners may

- Provide school-based therapists.
- Administer mental health screenings.
- Offer student, teacher, or parent mental health training.
- Connect families to mental health providers.
- Serve as the link to crisis support on the school district website.

Partners may also offer telehealth (virtual counseling) options for students. These may be provided by local care providers or national groups. The Cherry Creek School District, for example, partners with the national organization Hazel Health to offer telehealth services to families at no cost to them. Telehealth appointments may be available before, during, or after school. If appointments take place at school, trained school staff find a quiet place for the student to access the appointment with a tablet.

Nonprofit organizations also provide mental health services to schools. MindPeace is a nonprofit that leads a school-based mental health network based in Cincinnati, Ohio, that currently serves 250 urban, suburban, and rural schools in Ohio. MindPeace assists schools in identifying mental health issues specific to their communities and facilitates the selection of a lead mental health partner that is colocated at each school. MindPeace collaborates with those partner organizations to provide schools with a continuum of mental health care that ranges from therapy to medication management. MindPeace also provides targeted consultative support to enhance student wellness based on school needs. In collaboration with 1N5, a suicide prevention organization, MindPeace offers extensive resources such as a speaker series of videos and webinars for parents, teachers, and youth, and it sponsors community-wide in-person events like Family Education Day.

Local education foundations are another resource to fund student mental health. In Colorado, there are two such school district foundations: the Littleton Public Schools Foundation in Littleton and the Cherry Creek Schools Foundation in the Denver metropolitan area. The Littleton Public Schools Foundation works with mental health partners and community members to connect families with services. "What we really needed to do was create a network and connect families—remove the barriers of travel and language," said Nate Thompson, the director of social, emotional, and behavior services (Superville, 2023b). The foundation's list of therapists includes the languages each therapist speaks and their specialties. The foundation also raises money for emergency mental health treatment, workshops for parents, and the student mental health leadership advisory committee that gives feedback on student well-being issues.

The Cherry Creek Schools Foundation raises and distributes funds to many important school initiatives, including mental health services. Funds have been used to provide culturally responsive mental health care, crisis support, and grief counseling. Funding also allows families to connect with therapists outside the district and pay for therapy when families demonstrate financial need. The district has developed a network of more than 30 therapists who specialize in different areas like addiction and eating disorders (Superville, 2023b). The Cherry Creek Schools Foundation also partners with Servicios de La Raza (https://serviciosdelaraza.org), a nonprofit that provides essential services to the Latino community and refugees, with a special focus on the underserved and uninsured.

Even without foundations or partnerships, many schools are able to fund their student mental health programs through a patchwork of numerous state and federal grants. They may use federal title money or other federal grants such as School-Based Mental Health Services (SBMH) or Substance Abuse and Mental Health Services Administration (SAMHSA) grants. (For a list of federal grants for student mental health, see https://www.nea.org/resource-library/school-based-mental-health-services-grants or ed.gov.)

Wellness Needs Knowledge

As of this writing, 49 U.S. states and the District of Columbia require school personnel training for suicide prevention. This training is, at best, the bare minimum of training that teachers and staff should receive. Mental health training should include so much more. If student wellness takes a village, then everyone in the village needs knowledge to be able to do their part. Teachers, school staff, students, and parents all need mental health literacy education—basic knowledge of mental health disorders such as anxiety and depression, how to recognize signs of mental health problems in themselves and others, how to support those who are struggling, and how to refer them for specialized help. Providing this training for teachers, staff, students, and parents shows students that we value and prioritize mental health. It raises awareness about mental health and helps students see mental health as just one component of overall health like nutrition, sleep, and physical activity (Estrada & Popp, 2024). And it normalizes the idea of seeking help, just as one would for physical health problems. As the stated goal of the suicide prevention organization 1N5 puts it, "Stop the stigma. Start the conversation." This is where school foundations, local partners, and nonprofits can be especially useful. They may offer mental health training, refer the school district to groups that offer it, or provide funds to hire other agencies. Mental health literacy training is widely available through a number of national programs.

Teacher, Staff, and Parent Education

One of the most widely used mental health literacy training programs is Mental Health First Aid (https://www.mentalhealthfirstaid.org), an evidence-based course that has trained thousands of teachers. The program teaches people how to recognize signs of a mental health or substance abuse problem, how to respond, and how to encourage the individual to seek help from a mental health professional.

The American Psychiatric Association Foundation (APAF) offers free training for teachers and school staff. Its K–12 school staff training, *Notice. Talk. Act. at School* (apaf.org/schools), provides adults with evidence-based knowledge and skills to help them *notice* which behaviors could indicate a mental health issue, *talk* to students, and *act* or refer students to additional resources. APAF is currently developing a peer module and a family/caregiver module to be used in schools.

Many districts also offer education to parents about mental health and their role in their child's well-being. Olentangy Schools has a Parent Academy that offers education for parents on topics that support student academic success and well-being, such as the workshop *Mental Health 101: Introduction to and Understanding Mental Health in Children and Adolescents*. The district also offers a detailed program on digital wellness, teaching parents about the impact of social media; what to know about websites, games, and apps; and parental control software for their child's digital devices.

Student Education

Mental health knowledge is power, giving students the tools to take control of their mental health and to feel competent doing so. Just like their teachers and parents, students need mental health literacy—knowledge of mental health disorders, signs of mental health struggles in themselves and others, and when to reach out for help.

Adolescents also need media literacy training, which many states now require and many schools are now offering (Carrillo, 2023). The virtual world can be a useful source of information for adolescents who may be struggling with mental health conditions, but unfortunately, it can lead teens to erroneously self-diagnose serious conditions. As an example, an adolescent may seek mental health information on the internet and then decide that they are bipolar, even though what they are experiencing are the normal ups and downs of adolescence. Media literacy helps teens distinguish among reputable medical advice, personal opinions, and commercial sites selling supplements claiming to treat or cure mental health conditions. As one concerned educator said, "TikTok is their WebMD."

In addition to mental health literacy and media literacy, students also need to know how to stay physically and mentally well. That requires them to understand the sensitive nature of adolescent bodies and brains, and how each can affect the other. Science, health, or physical education classes are a logical place to discuss the relationship between stress and physical habits such as nutrition, sleep, and exercise.

Finally, students also need space to discover which restorative strategies help them de-stress, such as listening to music, spending time in nature, interacting with animals, or engaging in their favorite hobbies. Many schools provide information about restorative strategies through wellness seminars or wellness fairs, informed by student input and often led by mental health professionals in the building.

When schools plan and conduct wellness activities, they send the message to students that they care about their well-being, that it is worth prioritizing, and that they value mental health as an important part of overall health. The wellness center at Westlake High School hosts Wellness Wednesdays, seminars on mental health and well-being. Topics suggested by students have included toxic relationships, food and mood, and talking to parents (Superville, 2023a).

Another method of educating students about the importance of health and wellness is through a wellness fair. Wellness fairs show students that mental health is so important that time will be taken out of the school day to prioritize it. Wellness fairs are typically planned for half of a school day or an entire day in a workshop mode, where students sign up for various sessions they are interested in. At Cooperative Middle School in Stratham, New Hampshire, two teachers, Kelly Moss and Kelly O'Neill, have been organizing and supervising all the details of Health and Wellness Day for several years. With input from staff, students, and the community, they contact their PTA and local businesses for volunteers and create a list of sessions. To support all areas of wellness, workshops are offered by staff and local community members, college athletes, small business owners, and parents. Students select three sessions in advance, so a schedule can be created, and everyone knows where students are supposed to be. The day starts with a youth motivational speaker, and then students attend their three sessions. The sessions cover a wide range of wellness activities, from healthy eating and sleeping strategies to understanding anxiety to mindfulness and meditation to restorative activities such as journaling and arts and crafts. Some of the workshops that have been offered include the following (categorized by area of wellness):

- *Emotional wellness:* Meditation, mindfulness, sleeping strategies, understanding anxiety
- *Environmental wellness:* Photography, schoolwide clean-up, survival skills
- *Financial wellness:* Cash apps and fraud, investing, sustainability
- *Intellectual wellness:* Coding, holographic robots, jigsaw puzzles
- *Occupational wellness:* Forensic science, lifeguarding, ropes course maintenance, STEAM
- *Physical wellness:* Healthy eating, skills and drills, strength training, walking, yoga
- *Social wellness:* Arts and crafts, karaoke, theater
- *Spiritual wellness:* Journaling, meditation, mindfulness, vision boards, yoga

The feedback from students is always positive—they enjoy learning new things, making new friends, and finding new interests. After Health and Wellness Day, event photos are shared in news articles and the community newsletter. "Wellness Day is a transformative experience for our school community, offering students and staff a much-needed opportunity to recharge, reconnect, and focus on self-care. The day's activities are thoughtfully designed to foster relaxation, reflection, and a sense of personal well-being, creating a supportive and rejuvenating atmosphere for all," said the school's principal.

Littleton Public Schools has taken student mental health education and wellness to a whole new level by creating its own curriculum. As Meredith Henry, one of the LPS mental health coordinators, said, "We scanned the landscape and looked for a social-emotional curriculum that was brain-based, energizing for kids, and relevant for kids. We didn't find it and so we thought, let's make it ourselves."

The mental health coordinators took on the ambitious task of developing their own wellness curriculum for their middle and high school students. The three-year project was funded by a variety of grants along with the Littleton Public Schools Foundation and supported by a multidisciplinary task force of staff, students, and parents. Students helped pick topics, gave feedback to the graphic designers, and recorded student stories to be included in the lessons. The result of this effort was Mental Notes, a digital wellness curriculum with two versions—one tailored for middle school students and one for high school students. The brain-based series of short digital lessons features simple language, engaging graphics, and built-in student activities. It begins with a lesson on basic brain research, followed by lessons on such topics as the science of stress, the power of sleep, and the impact of social media and screen time, each connecting back to brain chemistry and the specific needs of adolescents. Teachers facilitate the lessons and the processing activities and, in doing so, are also educated. Mental Notes is now required curriculum for all 6th and 9th graders in the district.

Conclusion

Creating a school environment that nurtures student well-being is an ambitious undertaking. It requires us to build a foundation incorporating student voice; to structure a schedule that integrates academic, social, and autonomous time; and to provide mental health support and education. With time and commitment, the school community can become a village that looks and feels different from a traditional school—and is very much what our students need.

Afterword

Teen stress is a pervasive problem that requires complex solutions, but as educators, we can do our part to reduce school-related stress by honoring the developmental and human needs of adolescents. Here are just a few ways we can improve our students' day-to-day school experience and well-being:

- We can give students time and space to interact with their peers, both in and out of the classroom.
- We can allow students to have input into decisions in the school that affect them.
- We can give students autonomy in what and how they learn, and how they demonstrate that learning.
- We can educate students and their teachers about mental health.
- We can normalize mental health support within the school, so it becomes as common and acceptable as tutoring or visiting the school nurse.
- We can surround students with a community of caring adults, peers, and mental health professionals.

The schools featured in this book have demonstrated that these changes are possible. For all of them, it took time and commitment and some trial and error, as it would in any school or district. Implementing all the practices shared in this book would be an ambitious long-term initiative, but that should not deter you. Maybe it's not possible for your school to do *everything* described here, but your school can do *something*. You just need to begin. Don't your students deserve that?

Acknowledgments

My thanks go out first to Genny Ostertag, who encouraged the initial concept of the book and waited patiently for me to make the commitment to write it. Throughout its development, she saw things I didn't see, offered new perspectives, and reassured me when my confidence was shaky. I am grateful for her steadfast support. My thanks also to Miriam Calderone, who understood what I wanted to say, helped me to say it clearly, and smoothed the rough edges from my sometimes irreverent style.

This book would not be possible without the contributions of numerous teachers and administrators—some whom I seemed to meet at just the right time, some whom I stumbled upon or was led to, and all of whom became colleagues and friends. They gave unselfishly of their time, expertise, and guidance. They taught me things I needed to know and gave my research direction. I am so grateful for them.

A special thanks to Steve Nederveld, a mental health professional who, more than anyone else, showed me the big picture of the depth and breadth of student support that a school system could provide. Thanks also to Mike Nicholson and Nathan Gorsch, who taught me what true student autonomy looks like and who connected me to the innovative educators in the Learning Inspired network of schools.

Next, thanks to the many psychologists, pediatricians, counselors, therapists, and other mental health professionals who graciously agreed to be interviewed for this book. Their expertise and perspectives were invaluable, and they provided me with a much-needed window into the complexities of adolescent mental health.

And last, thanks to my husband Glenn, who patiently tolerated bouts of writer's block, dinners alone when the ideas were flowing freely, and the ever-present manuscript on family vacations.

References

Abeles, V. (2015). *Beyond measure: Rescuing an overscheduled, overtested, underestimated generation.* Simon & Schuster.

American Academy of Pediatrics. (2021). *A declaration from the American Academy of Pediatrics, American Academy of Child and Adolescent Psychiatry and Children's Hospital Association.* https://www.aap.org/en/advocacy/child-and-adolescent-healthy-mental-development/aap-aacap-cha-declaration-of-a-national-emergency-in-child-and-adolescent-mental-health/

American Psychological Association (APA). (2018). *Helicopter parenting may negatively affect children's emotional well-being, behavior.* https://www.apa.org/news/press/releases/2018/06/helicopter-parenting

American Student Assistance. (2025). *Next steps: An analysis of teens' post-high school plans.* https://www.asa.org/research/teens-next-steps-report-2025

Anderson, M. (2016). *Learning to choose, choosing to learn: The key to student motivation and achievement.* ASCD.

Anderson, M. (2021). *Tackling the motivation crisis: How to activate student learning without behavior charts, pizza parties, or other hard-to-quit incentive systems.* ASCD.

Armstrong, T. (2016). *The power of the adolescent brain: Strategies for teaching middle and high school students.* ASCD.

Banerji, O. (2025). What schools look like without the cellphone distraction. *Education Week, 44*(18), 8–9.

Belkin, D. (2024, October 15). The guru who says he can get your 11-year-old into Harvard. *Wall Street Journal.* https://www.wsj.com/us-news/education/ivy-league-college-venture-capital-23dc95fa?st=Ucdgcb

Benson, J. (2019). When rules get in the way. *Educational Leadership, 76*(8), 34–39.

Brooks, D. (2023). *How to know a person: The art of seeing others deeply and being deeply seen.* Random House.

Brooks, D. (2024). How the Ivy League broke America. *The Atlantic, 334*(5), 26–40.

Brooks, R., & Goldstein, S. (2001). *Raising resilient children: Fostering strength, happiness, and optimism in your child.* McGraw-Hill.

Bruni, F. (2016). *Where you go is not who you'll be: An antidote to the college admissions mania.* Grand Central Publishing.

Burg, X., Metcalfe, J. J., Ellison, B., & Prescott, M. P. (2021). Effects of longer seated lunch time on food consumption and waste in elementary and middle school-age children: A randomized clinical trial. *JAMA Network Open, 4*(6). https://jamanetwork.com/journals/jamanetworkopen/fullarticle/2781214

Calderon, V. J., & Yu, D. (2016). Student enthusiasm falls as high school graduation nears. https://news.gallup.com/opinion/gallup/211631/student-enthusiasm-falls-high-school-graduation-nears.aspx

Carrillo, S. (Reporter). (2023, November 24). California joins a growing movement to teach media literacy in schools [Radio show episode]. *All things considered.* NPR. https://www.npr.org/2023/11/24/1215152769/california-joins-a-growing-movement-to-teach-media-literacy-in-schools

Centers for Disease Control and Prevention (CDC). (2019). *Youth risk behavior survey: Data summary and trends report 2009–2019.* https://www.cdc.gov/healthyyouth/data/yrbs/pdf/YRBSDataSummaryTrendsReport2019-508.pdf

Centers for Disease Control and Prevention (CDC). (2024). *Sleep in middle and high school students.* https://www.cdc.gov/healthyschools/features/students-sleep.htm

Challenge Success. (2021, June 4). *Time management for students.* Stanford Graduate School of Education. https://challengesuccess.org/resources/time-management

Challenge Success & NBC News. (2021, February). *Kids under pressure: A look at student well-being and engagement during the pandemic.* https://challengesuccess.org/wp-content/uploads/2021/02/CS-NBC-Study-Kids-Under-Pressure-PUBLISHED.pdf

Crouch, E., Radcliff, E., Probst, J. C., Bennett, K. J., & McKinney, S. H. (2020, January). Rural-urban differences in adverse childhood experiences across a national sample of children. *Journal of Rural Health, 36*(1), 55–64.

DeAngelis, T. (2024). Teens are spending nearly 5 hours daily on social media. Here are the mental health outcomes. *Monitor on Psychology, 55*(3), 80.

Eccles, J. (2024, November 7). *Creating space for student voice at the leadership level.* Presentation at the Association for Middle Level Education Annual Conference.

Estrada, J-D., & Popp, S. (2024, February 1). 4 pillars of school mental health. *Educational Leadership, 81*(5), 32–37.

Faverio, M., & Sidoti, O. (2024, December 12). *Teens, social media and technology 2024.* Pew Research Center. https://www.pewresearch.org/internet/2024/12/12/teens-social-media-and-technology-2024

Feldman, J. (2019). *Grading for equity: What it is, why it matters, and how it can transform schools and classrooms.* Corwin.

Flanagan, C. (2021, April). Private schools are indefensible. *The Atlantic.* https://www.theatlantic.com/magazine/archive/2021/04/private-schools-are-indefensible/618078/

Fullan, M. (2021). *The right drivers for whole system success: CSE Leading Education Series #1.* Centre for Strategic Education.

Gall, G., Pagano, M. E., Desmond, M. S., Perrin, J. M., & Murphy, J. M. (2000, September). Utility of psychosocial screening at a school-based health center. *Journal of School Health, 70*(7), 292–298.

Gewertz, C. (2022, March 1). Peer help for mental health: "We learn the red flags to watch for." *Education Week.* https://www.edweek.org/leadership/peer-help-for-mental-health-we-learn-the-red-flags-to-watch-for/2022/03

Glasser, W. (1992). *The quality school: Managing students without coercion.* Harper & Row.

Goldstein, D., & Healy, J. (2019, March 13). Inside the pricey, totally legal world of college consultants. *New York Times.* https://www.nytimes.com/2019/03/13/us/admissions-cheating-scandal-consultants.html

Gray, P., Lancy, D. F., & Bjorklund, D. F. (2023). Decline in independent activity as a cause of decline in children's mental well-being: Summary of the evidence. *Journal of Pediatrics, 260*(2).

Hafen, C. A., Allen, J. P., Mikami, A. Y., Gregory, A., Hamre, B., & Pianta, R. C. (2012, March). The pivotal role of adolescent autonomy in secondary school classrooms. *Journal of Youth and Adolescence, 41*(3), 245–255.

Haidt, J. (2024). *The anxious generation: How the great rewiring of childhood is causing an epidemic of mental illness.* Penguin.

Hall, G. S. (1904). *Adolescence: Its psychology and its relations to physiology, anthropology, sociology, sex, crime, religion, and education.* D. Appleton.

Hall, H. R. (2019). What do black adolescents need from school? *Educational Leadership, 76*(8), 52–57.

Hargreaves, A., & Shirley, D. (2022). *Well-being in schools: Three forces that will uplift your students in a volatile world.* ASCD.

Hari, J. (2018). *Lost connections: Uncovering the real causes of depression—and the unexpected solutions.* Bloomsbury.

Hill, N. E., & Redding, A. (2021). *The end of adolescence: The lost art of delaying adulthood.* Harvard University Press.

Horowitz, J. M., Igielnik, R., & Kochar, R. (2020). *Trends in income and wealth inequality.* Pew Research Center. https://www.pewresearch.org/social-trends/2020/01/09/trends-in-income-and-wealth-inequality

Jacobson, R., Bubrick, J., Dubinski, A., & Ruggiero, S. (2025). *Should kids take mental health days? When taking a break is helpful and when it's not.* Child Mind Institute. https://childmind.org/article/should-kids-take-mental-health-days

Jana, T., & Baran, M. (2020). *Subtle acts of exclusion: How to understand, identify, and stop microaggressions.* Berrett-Koehler.

Jellinek, M., & Murphy, J. M. (1988). Pediatric Symptom Checklist (youth self-report version). Massachusetts General Hospital. https://www.massgeneral.org/psychiatry/treatments-and-services/pediatric-symptom-checklist

Jellinek, M. S., Murphy, J. M., Robinson, J., Feins, A., Lamb, S., & Fenton, T. (1988). Pediatric Symptom Checklist: Screening school-age children for psychosocial dysfunction. *The Journal of Pediatrics, 112*(2), 201–209.

Jensen, E. (2000). *Brain-based learning.* The Brain Store.

Kallick, B., & Zmuda, A. (2017). *Students at the center: Personalized learning with habits of mind.* ASCD.

Keels, M. (2023). *Trauma responsive educational practices: Helping students cope and learn.* ASCD.

Kittle, P., & Gallagher, K. (2020). The curse of "helicopter teaching." *Educational Leadership, 77*(6), 15–19.

Klein, A. (2021, October 12). The pandemic has shaken students' sense of themselves. *Education Week.* https://www.edweek.org/leadership/the-pandemic-has-shaken-students-sense-of-themselves/2021/10

Lahey, J. (2015). *The gift of failure: How the best parents learn to let go so their children can succeed.* HarperCollins.

Langreo, L., & Prothero, A. (2025). More states are moving to ban cellphones at school. Should they? *Education Week, 44*(18), pp. 8–9.

Levine, M. (2006). *The price of privilege: How parental pressure and material advantage are creating a generation of disconnected and unhappy kids.* HarperCollins.

Lieberman, M. (2023, February 6). Giving students a say in school spending? A district leader's bold idea pays off. *Education Week.* https://www.edweek.org/leaders/2023/giving-students-a-say-in-school-spending-a-district-leaders-bold-idea-pays-off

Lythcott-Haims, J. (2015). *How to raise an adult: Break free of the overparenting trap and prepare your kids for success.* Henry Holt.

Massachusetts General Hospital Department of Psychiatry. (n.d.). Pediatric Symptom Checklist. https://www.massgeneral.org/psychiatry/treatments-and-services/pediatric-symptom-checklist

Mayo Clinic. (2024). *Teens and social media use: What's the impact?* https://www.mayoclinic.org/healthy-lifestyle/tween-and-teen-health/in-depth/teens-and-social-media-use/art-20474437

McDougal, J. L., Bardos, A. N., & Meier, S. T. (2020). Behavior Intervention Monitoring Assessment System (BIMAS-2). Edumetrisis. https://edumetrisis.com/bimas-2

McTighe, J., & Tucker, C. (2022). Developing self-directed learners by design. *Educational Leadership, 80*(3), 58–64.

Melito-Connors, T. (2024). The second backpack: Creating predictable systems for students with trauma. *Educational Leadership, 81*(5), 20–25.

Miles, S., Pope, D., Villeneuve, J. C., & Selby, S. T. (2022, Summer). Making time for well-being. *Educational Leadership, 79*(9), 60–65.

Miller, C. C. (2018, December 12). The relentlessness of modern parenting. *New York Times*. https://nytimes.com/2018/12/25/upshot/the-relentless-of-modern-parenting.html

National Association for College Admission Counseling. (2024, August). *Guide to ethical practice in college admission*. https://www.nacacnet.org/who-we-are/what-we-do/guiding-ethics/nacacs-guide-to-ethical-practice-in-college-admission

National Center for School Mental Health. (2025). *School Health Assessment and Performance Evaluation System*. https://www.schoolmentalhealth.org/shape

National Institute of Mental Health. (2022). *Suicide is one of the leading causes of death in the United States*. https://www.nimh.nih.gov/health/statistics/suicide

National Institutes of Health. (2020, November 10). *Rural youth often lack access to suicide prevention resources*. https://www.nih.gov/news-events/nih-research-matters/rural-youth-often-lack-access-suicide-prevention-services

National Research Council, Institute of Medicine Forum on Adolescence, & Graham, M. G. (Ed.). (2000). *Sleep needs, patterns, and difficulties of adolescents: Summary of a workshop*. National Academies Press. https://www.ncbi.nlm.nih.gov/books/NBK222804

National Sleep Foundation. (2022, March 13). *Screen use disrupts precious sleep time*. https://www.thensf.org/screen-use-disrupts-precious-sleep-time

National Sleep Foundation. (2024, March 7). *The critical connection between teens' sleep and mental health*. https://www.thensf.org/the-critical-connection-between-teens-sleep-and-mental-health/

Niemiec, C. P., & Ryan, R. M. (2009). Autonomy, competence, and relatedness in the classroom: Applying self-determination theory to educational practice. *Theory and Research in Education, 7*(2), 133–144.

Novotney, A. (2009, January). The price of affluence. *Monitor on Psychology, 40*(1), 50. https://www.apa.org/monitor/2009/01/teens

Peetz, C. (2024, August 21). Do students think what they're learning matters? *Education Week*. https://www.edweek.org/leadership/do-students-think-what-theyre-learning-matters/2024/08

Pink, D. H. (2009). *Drive: The surprising truth about what motivates us*. Riverhead Books.

Pope, D. (2016, December 15). *What parents say matters*. Challenge Success. https://challengesuccess.org/resources/parents-say-matters

Prothero, A. (2023, January 19). More schools are offering mental health days: Here's what you need to know. *Education Week*. https://www.edweek.org/leadership/more-schools-are-offering-student-mental-health-days-heres-what-you-need-to-know/2023/01

Ramey, G., & Ramey V. A. (2009, August). *The rug rat race*. (NBER Working Paper No. 15284). National Bureau of Economic Research. http://www.nber.org/papers/w15284

Samuels, C. A. (2020, March 3). Sleep helps teens cope with stress; instances of discrimination, study finds. *Education Week*. https://www.edweek.org/leadership/sleep-helps-teens-cope-with-stress-instances-of-discrimination-study-finds/2020/03

Schrobsdorff, S. (2016, November 7). Teen depression and anxiety: Why the kids are not alright. *Time, 188*(19), 44–51.

Sparks, S. D., & Prothero, A. (2023, September 20). Teachers say students don't have enough time to eat lunch. Here's how to change that. *Education Week.* https://www.edweek.org/leadership/teachers-say-students-dont-have-enough-time-to-eat-lunch-heres-how-to-change-that/2023/09

Stanford, L. (2023, February 6). A "saleslady" got one district to prioritize students' mental health. *Education Week.* https://www.edweek.org/leaders/2023/a-saleslady-got-one-district-to-prioritize-students-mental-health

Steinberg, L. (2014). *Age of opportunity: Lessons from the new science of adolescence.* Mariner.

Steinberg, L. (2017). *Adolescence* (11th ed.). McGraw-Hill.

Steiner, R. J., Sheremenko, G., Lesesne, C., Dittus, P. J., Sieving, R. E., & Ethier, K. A. (2019, July 1). Adolescent connectedness and adult health outcomes. *Pediatrics, 144*(1). https://publications.aap.org/pediatrics/article-abstract/144/1/e20183766/37106/Adolescent-Connectedness-and-Adult-Health-Outcomes

Stixrud, W., & Johnson, N. (2018). *The self-driven child: The science and sense of giving your kids more control over their lives.* Penguin.

Stone, M. (2024a, April 14). Relationships matter: Building strong student-school connections. *Education Week, 43*(24). https://www.edweek.org/leadership/relationships-matter-building-strong-student-school-connections

Stone, M. (2024b, April 14). "A universal prevention measure" that boosts attendance and improves behavior. *Education Week, 43*(24), 3–6.

Stone, M. (2024c, April 14). 4 case studies: Schools use connections to give every student a reason to attend. *Education Week, 43*(24), 7–10.

Suni, E. (2023, October 4). *Teens and sleep.* National Sleep Foundation. https://www.sleepfoundation.org/teens-and-sleep

Superville, D. R. (2023a, February 24). Zen dens: Creating mental health spaces at school. *Education Week.* https://www.edweek.org/leadership/zen-dens-creating-mental-health-spaces-at-school/2023/02

Superville, D. R. (2023b, January 23). School foundations shift their focus to students' mental health as need grows. *Education Week.* https://www.edweek.org/leadership/school-foundations-shift-their-focus-to-students-mental-health-as-need-grows/2023/01

Thompson, D. (2022, April 11). Why American teens are so sad. *The Atlantic.* https://www.theatlantic.com/newsletters/archive/2022/04/american-teens-sadness-depression-anxiety/629524

Twenge, J. M. (2018). *iGen: Why today's kids are growing up less rebellious, more tolerant, less happy—and completely unprepared for adulthood.* Atria.

Twenge, J. M., Cooper, A., Bell, J., Thomas, E., Duffy, M. E., & Binau, S. G. (2019, April). Age, period, and cohort trends in mood disorder indicators and suicide-related outcomes in a nationally representative dataset, 2005–2017. *Journal of Abnormal Psychology, 128*(3), 185–199.

Twenge, J. M., Gentile, B., DeWall, C. N., Ma, D., Lacefield, K., & Schurtz, D. R. (2010, March). Birth cohort increases in psychopathology among young

Americans, 1938–2007: A cross-temporal meta-analysis of the MMPI. *Clinical Psychology Review, 30*(2), 145–154.

U.S. Surgeon General. (2021). *Protecting youth mental health: The U.S. Surgeon General's Advisory.* https://www.hhs.gov/sites/default/files/surgeon-general-youth-mental-health-advisory.pdf

Vatterott, C. (2007). *Becoming a middle level teacher: Student-focused teaching of early adolescents.* McGraw-Hill.

Vatterott, C. (2015). *Rethinking grading: Meaningful assessment for standards-based learning.* ASCD.

Vatterott, C. (2017). One-size-doesn't-fit-all homework. *Educational Leadership, 74*(6), 34–39.

Vatterott, C. (2018). *Rethinking homework: Best practices that support diverse needs* (2nd ed.). ASCD.

Vatterott, C. (2019). The teens are not alright. *Educational Leadership, 76*(8), 13–16.

Vatterott, C. (2022). Lessons on student well-being from "the great resignation." *Educational Leadership, 79*(9), 26–30.

Vatterott, C. (2024). Student mental health: What's autonomy got to do with it? *Educational Leadership, 81*(5), 62–66.

Wiliam, D. (2007). Content *then* process: Teacher learning communities in the service of formative assessment. In D. Reeves (Ed.), *Ahead of the curve: The power of assessment to transform teaching and learning* (pp. 183–206). Solution Tree.

Index

Note: Page references followed by an italicized *f* indicates information contained in a figure.

absenteeism, 88, 94–95
abstract thinking, 19
abuse and neglect, 77
academic dishonesty, 88
academic lab, 82
academic learning, student well-being and, 31
academic obsession, 10, 15
academic time, 81–82
acceptance, 32
achievement culture, 9–11, 12, 24, 34–36
addiction, 28
advanced placement (AP) classes, 12, 15, 86
advisory periods, 82, 84, 92–93
affiliation, 26
affirmation, 32
affluent families
    achievement culture, 9–11, 34–36
    and college admissions industry, 11–15
    depression and anxiety disorders, 2
    wealth gap, 8–11
    wellness paradigm shift, 34–36
American Academy of Child and Adolescent Psychiatry, 1
American Academy of Pediatrics, 1, 96
American Psychiatric Association Foundation (APAF), 103
anxiety, 2, 17

The Anxious Generation: How the Great Rewiring of Childhood Is Causing an Epidemic of Mental Illness (Haidt), 4–5
apathy, 56
assessment of learning, 58, 63, 73–74. *See also* grading practices
attendance monitoring, 88, 94–95
autonomous time, 84–85
autonomy
    adolescent need for, 31–32, 55–56
    in schools, 38, 51
    in student learning, 57–66, 59*f,* 60*f*–61*f*

bad news bias, 4
Basehor-Linwood High School (Kansas), 64–65
Beaton, Jamie, 13
becoming, 31–32
behavioral challenges, 2
behavior control, 50–54
Behavior Intervention Monitoring Assessment System (BIMAS-2), 96, 97*f*
belonging, 46–50, 94–95
biology
    body biology during adolescence, 16–18
    brain development, 18–19
    of sleep, 17–18

Index

blue light, 17
body biology during adolescence, 16–18
brain development, 18–19
Bruni, Frank, 13
bulldozer parenting, 6–8
bullying, 94–95

caffeine, 17
capstone experiences, 63–64
career education, 36
Caryl-Klika, Jaime, 13
Challenge Success, 85
Cherry Creek School District (Denver), 91, 98, 100
Cherry Creek Schools Foundation (Denver), 101
Children's Hospital Association, 1
Choose a Trusted Adult program, 92
circadian rhythms, 17–18
classroom practices and policies
    challenges, 72–74
    collaboration, 54
    grading practices, 40, 66–69
    homework practices, 40, 69–72
    norms, 52–53
    relationship prioritization and belonging, 46–50
    routines, 53–54
    student-student relationships, 47–50
    student voice, 55–66, 59f, 60f–61f
    teacher-student relationships, 47–50
    in wellness paradigm, 38, 39–40, 41f
CNN, 3, 6
collaboration, 38, 52–54
college admissions industry, 11–15, 24, 25
college consultants, 12–13
Colleyville Middle School (Texas), 92
community, 32
competence, 31–32, 38
competence, islands of, 20–22
concrete thinking, 19
conditional love, 24
connectedness, 32
Connect Time, 85
content of learning, 58, 63
Cooperative Middle School (New Hampshire), 104–105
coping strategies, 42
cortisol, 18
COVID-19 pandemic, 1, 47
crisis support, 99–100
culminating projects, 63–64
cultural influences on teen stress
    about, 1–3
    achievement culture, 9–11, 12

cultural influences on teen stress (*continued*)
    college admissions industry, 11–15
    decline of independent play, 8
    media overload, 3–4
    parenting trends, 6–8
    smartphones and social media, 4–6
    wealth gap, 8–11

decision making, 17, 18, 38, 78–80
depression, 17, 99
developmental needs, 19
    identity development, 20
    independence from parents, 23–25
    islands of competence, 20–22
    peer relationships, 25–26
    and school, 28–29
    and the virtual world, 26–28
dignity, 46–47
distance learning, 86
dopamine, 18, 28
dual rubrics, 74

early dismissal days, 86
educational foundations, 100–102
emergency room visits, 2
emotional brain, 18
emotional wellness workshops, 105
engagement, student, 55–57
environmental wellness workshops, 105
equitable grading practices, 88, 89
Erikson, Erik, 19
ethnicity
    belonging and, 46
    ethnic identity, 20
executive functioning, 17, 18
exercise, 17

Facebook, 5
fail, freedom to, 7–8
financial wellness workshops, 105
flex time, 83–84
formative assessment, 69, 88–89
4x4 semesters, 86
Frederick County Public Schools (Virginia), 58–65, 59f, 60f–61f

gender identity, 20, 46
Generation Z, 5
genius hour projects, 64
girls, self-esteem and perfectionism, 21, 24, 27
goal, learning, 58, 63
grading practices, 40, 66–70, 88. *See also* assessment of learning
guiding lights, 32

Haidt, Jonathan, 4–5
Hall, G. Stanley, 29
Hardin Middle School (Missouri), 79, 83
Hazel Health, 100
healthy habits, 17
helicopter parenting, 6–8
Henry, Meredith, 105–106
Hilliard Davidson High School (Ohio), 93–94
homework practices, 40, 69–72, 88–89
Hope Squad, 93–94
hormones, 16–17

identity development, 6, 20, 35
impulse control, 18
independence from parents, 23–25
independent play, 8
Innovation Academy, 64–65, 74
Instagram, 5
intellectual wellness workshops, 105
interdisciplinary teams, 90
islands of competence, 20–22
Ivy League, 10, 11

James E. Dottke High School (Wisconsin), 85

language, and belonging, 46
late-start days, 86
leadership, 38
learning
    components of, 58
    experience of process of, 39–40, 41*f*
    student autonomy and, 57–66, 59*f*, 60*f*–61*f*
learning preferences, 73
Learning to Choose, Choosing to Learn: The Key to Student Motivation and Achievement (Anderson), 62
limbic system, 18
Littleton Public Schools (Colorado), 93, 105–106
Littleton Public Schools Foundation (Colorado), 101
long-term project grading, 67
lunch period, 81

major depression, 2
maladaptive perfectionism, 24
Mattoon Middle School (Illinois), 81, 85, 92, 95
media literacy training, 103
media overload, 3–4, 6–7
Mental Health 101: Introduction to and Understanding Mental Health in Children and Adolescents, 103
mental health days, student, 95–96
Mental Health First Aid, 102

mental health support experience, school, 41–43, 43*f*. *See also* schoolwide wellness practices, policies, and programs
mental health training, 102–106
mentor programs, 92
MindPeace, 100–101
mirrors, 32
mood, 17
Moss, Kelly, 104–105

National Center for School Mental Health at the University of Maryland School of Medicine, 99
needs, student psychological, 31–32
nonacademic time, 82–83
nonfatal self-harm, 2
norms, classroom, 52–53
Notice. Talk. Act. at School, 103
nutrition, 17

occupational wellness workshops, 105
Olentangy Schools (Ohio), 99, 103
1N5, 101
O'Neill, Kelly, 104–105
One Trusted Adult program, 92

parents
    expectations and values, 23–25
    mental health training, 102–103
    parenting trends, 6–8
    permissions for wellness screening, 98–99
partnerships, 100–102
passing time, 81
passion projects, 64
Pediatric Symptom Checklist (PSC), 97, 98*f*
peer approval, 6
peer evaluation, 67
peer relationships and development, 25–26, 32, 47–50, 93–94
perfectionism, 24
personalized learning, 59*f*, 63–66
Phoenix Union High School District, 79
physical wellness workshops, 105
planning, 18
play, 8
policy as wellness support, 87–89
postsecondary options, 36
poverty, 9
power structures, school, 36–39, 39*f*, 77, 78–80
practice tests, 67–68
prefrontal cortex, 18
problem solving, 17, 38
product, learning, 58, 63

Protecting Youth Mental Health (U.S. Surgeon General), 1
pruning (brain function), 18
psychosocial moratorium, 19

quizzes. *See* grading practices

race
    belonging and, 46
    racial identity, 20
relatedness, 31–32
relationships
    prioritization and belonging, 46–50
    student well-being and, 32
    as support, 92–94
relevance of content, 56–57
religion, and belonging, 46
respect, 46–47
retakes, 68–69
rewards and punishments, 50
routines, classroom, 53–54
rubrics, 73–74
rug rat race, 14
rumination, 25–26
rural adolescence, 9

sadness and hopelessness, 2
schedule choices and changes, student, 85–86. *See also* time and scheduling
School-Based Mental Health Services (SBMH), 101
School Health Assessment and Performance Evaluation (SHAPE) System, 99
schools
    and adolescent developmental needs, 28–29
    learning process experience, 39–40, 41*f*
    mental health support experience, 41–43, 43*f*
    power structures, 36–39, 39*f*
    start times, 17–18
    student success definition, 34–36, 37*f*
    websites and crisis support, 99–100
schoolwide wellness practices, policies, and programs
    attendance monitoring, 94–95
    crisis support, 99–100
    partnerships and foundations, 100–102
    policy as wellness support, 87–89
    relationships as support, 92–94
    stress reduction and self-regulation programs, 90–92
    student mental health days, 95–96
    student mental health training, 103–106

schoolwide wellness practices, policies, and programs (*continued*)
    student voice and power, 78–80
    teacher, staff, and parent mental health training, 102–103
    time and scheduling, 80–86
    wellness screening, 96–99, 97*f*, 98*f*
    wellness support strategies, 86–102
    whole child approach, 77–78
    workload coordination across classes, 90
self-assessment, 67
self-determination theory, 31
self-esteem, 6, 21, 25, 27
self-regulation programs, 90–92
serotonin, 18
Servicios de La Raza, 101
sexual identity, 20, 46
Signs of Suicide (SOS), 98
sleep, biology of, 17–18
smartphones, 4–6, 28
social-emotional learning (SEL) self-assessment, 98
social interaction, 28, 47
social media
    and adolescent developmental, 26–28
    girls and, 27
    impact of, 4–6
    virtual world and developmental needs, 26–28
social wellness workshops, 105
Sources of Strength, 93
South View Middle School (Minnesota), 82, 83–84, 92–93
SPEAK (Students Promoting Emotional Awareness & Kindness), 93
spiritual wellness workshops, 105
staff mental health training, 102–103
standards-based grading, 88, 89
status insecurity, 10
"storm and strife," 29
strategy formation, 18
stress reduction programs, 90–92
student-centered learning, 59*f*, 62–63
student-directed learning, 59*f*, 63–66
student mental health days, 95–96
students
    engagement, 55–57
    importance of knowing names, 48
    media literacy training, 103
    peer approval, 6
    peer evaluation, 67
    peer relationships and development, 25–26, 32, 47–50, 93–94
    schedule choices and changes, 85–86

students (*continued*)
    self-assessment skills, 73–74
    self-direction skills, 72–73
    self-knowledge of learning preferences, 73
    teacher relationships, 47–50
    wellness training, 103–106
student voice
    and autonomy in learning, 57–66, 59*f*, 60*f*–61*f*
    in classroom rules and norms, 50–54
    engagement problem, 55–57
    as necessary for wellness, 78–80
student well-being, 30–31. *See also* wellness paradigm
    as necessary foundation for academic learning, 31
    as needs based, 31–32
    as relationship driven, 32
    takes a village, 33
Substance Abuse and Mental Health Services Administration (SAMHSA), 101–102
success definition, student, 34–36, 37*f*. *See also* achievement culture
suicide prevention training, 102
suicide rates
    10–14-year olds, 2
    rural adolescence, 9

teacher-centered learning, 59*f*, 62
teacher-directed learning, 59*f*, 62
teachers
    coordination across subjects, 72, 90
    mental health training, 102–103
    relationships with students, 47–50
teen mental health crisis, 1–3
telehealth, 100
tests. *See* grading practices
Thomas Kelly College Preparatory School (Chicago), 78
Thompson, Nate, 101
time and scheduling, 77, 80
    autonomous time, 84–85
    blocks of academic time, 81–82
    blocks of nonacademic time, 82–83
    flex time, 83–84
    passing time and lunch period, 81
    student schedule choices, 85–86
Traverse Academy, 100
24-hour news cycle, 3–4, 6–7
Twitter, 5

unconditional love, 24
unlockingtime.org, 86
urban adolescence, 9
U.S. Surgeon General, 1

validation, 32
village mentality, 33
Village School (Colorado), 80
virtual world and developmental needs, 26–28. *See also* social media

wealth gap, 8–11
wellness fairs, 104–105
wellness paradigm, 33–34. *See also* student well-being
    learning process experience, 39–40, 41*f*
    mental health support experience, 41–43, 43*f*
    power structures, 36–39, 39*f*
    success definition, 34–36, 37*f*
wellness practices, policies, and programs. *See* schoolwide wellness practices, policies, and programs
wellness screening, 96–99, 97*f*, 98*f*
wellness support strategies
    attendance monitoring, 94–95
    crisis support, 99–100
    partnerships and foundations, 100–102
    policy as wellness support, 87–89
    relationships as support, 92–94
    stress reduction and self-regulation programs, 90–92
    student mental health days, 95–96
    time and scheduling, 80 86
    wellness screening, 96–99, 97*f*, 98*f*
    workload coordination across classes, 90
Westlake High School (Utah), 91, 104
Where You Go Is Not Who You'll Be: An Antidote to the College Admissions Mania (Bruni), 13
whole child philosophy, 44
whole-class discussion, 67
William Mason High School (Ohio), 80, 94
windows, 32
WIN (What I Need) time, 81
workload coordination across classes, 90

Zen dens, 91

About the Author

Dr. Cathy Vatterott is Professor Emeritus of Education at the University of Missouri–St. Louis, a former middle school and high school teacher, and a former middle school principal. She is the author of two other ASCD books, *Rethinking Homework: Best Practices That Support Diverse Needs, 2nd Edition* (2018), and *Rethinking Grading: Meaningful Assessment for Standards-Based Learning* (2015). She frequently presents at national conferences and serves as a consultant to K–12 schools on the topics of homework and grading.

After working for several years with high-achieving secondary schools on homework and grading reform, Vatterott became alarmed at the level of student stress at those schools. That concern was the catalyst for her research and the impetus for writing this book.

She can be reached at vatterott@umsl.edu or through her website at www.homeworklady.com.

Related ASCD Resources

At the time of publication, the following resources were available (ASCD stock numbers appear in parentheses).

Attack of the Teenage Brain! Understanding and Supporting the Weird and Wonderful Adolescent Learner by John Medina (#118024)

From Stressed Out to Stress Wise: How You and Your Students Can Navigate Challenges and Nurture Vitality by Abby Wills, Anjali Deva, and Niki Saccareccia (#123004)

Learning to Choose, Choosing to Learn: The Key to Student Motivation and Achievement by Mike Anderson (#116015)

The Meaningful Middle School Classroom: How to Spark Engagement That Fosters Deep Learning by Jennifer Ciok (#125008)

The Power of the Adolescent Brain: Strategies for Teaching Middle and High School Students by Thomas Armstrong (#116017)

Rethinking Grading: Meaningful Assessment for Standards-Based Learning by Cathy Vatterott (#115001)

Rethinking Homework: Best Practices That Support Diverse Needs, 2nd Edition by Cathy Vatterott (#119001)

Students at the Center: Personalized Learning with Habits of Mind by Bena Kallick and Allison Zmuda (#117015)

Tackling the Motivation Crisis: How to Activate Student Learning Without Behavior Charts, Pizza Parties, or Other Hard-to-Quit Incentive Systems by Mike Anderson (#121033)

Trauma-Responsive Educational Practices: Helping Students Cope and Learn by Micere Keels (#122015)

Well-Being in Schools: Three Forces That Will Uplift Your Students in a Volatile World by Andy Hargreaves and Dennis Shirley (#122025)

For up-to-date information about ASCD resources, go to **www.ascd.org**. You can search the complete archives of *Educational Leadership* at **www.ascd.org/el.** To contact us, send an email to member@ascd.org or call 1-800-933-2723 or 703-578-9600.

DON'T MISS A SINGLE ISSUE OF THIS AWARD-WINNING MAGAZINE.

iste+ascd
educational leadership

If you belong to a Professional Learning Community, you may be looking for a way to get your fellow educators' minds around a complex topic. Why not delve into a relevant theme issue of *Educational Leadership*, the journal written by educators for educators?

Subscribe now and browse or purchase back issues of our flagship publication at **www.ascd.org/el**. Discounts on bulk purchases are available.

iste+ascd

Arlington, VA USA
1-800-933-2723

www.ascd.org
www.iste.org